# Arthur Bliss

Sir Arthur and Lady Bliss. By kind permission of G. MacDomnic, FRPS., ABIPP

# Arthur Bliss

## *A Bio-Bibliography*

### Stewart R. Craggs

Donald L. Hixon, Series Adviser

Bio-Bibliographies in Music,
Number 13

GREENWOOD PRESS
New York • Westport, Connecticut • London

**Library of Congress Cataloging-in-Publication Data**

Craggs, Stewart R.
  Arthur Bliss : a bio-bibliography / Stewart R. Craggs.
    p.  cm. — (Bio-bibliographies in music, ISSN 0742-6968 ; no. 13)
  Includes index.
  ISBN 0-313-25739-6 (lib. bdg. : alk. paper)
  1. Bliss, Arthur, Sir, 1891-1975—Bibliography.  2. Bliss, Arthur, Sir, 1891-1975—Discography.  3. Music—Bio-bibliography.
I. Title.  II. Series.
ML134.B62C7 1988
016.78'092'4—dc19                                88-10975

British Library Cataloguing in Publication Data is available.

Library of Congress Catalog Card Number: 88-10975
ISBN: 0-313-25739-6
ISSN: 0742-6968

First published in 1988

Greenwood Press, Inc.
88 Post Road West, Westport, Connecticut 06881

Printed in the United States of America

10 9 8 7 6 5 4 3 2 1

# Contents

# Preface

Sir Arthur Bliss was one of England's most famous twentieth century composers and an important Master of the Queen's Musick. He is therefore an excellent subject for the Greenwood Press composer bio-bibliography series.

The present volume consists of the following:

(1)  a short <u>biography</u>, prepared with the kind assistance of Lady Bliss;

(2)  a complete list of <u>works and performances</u>, classified by genre and then arranged alphabetically by title of composition. Following each title are details of a work's first and other selected performances, with references to commentaries from reviews listed in the "Bibliography." Each work is prefaced by a mnemonic "W" and each performance of that work is identified by successive lower case letters. As will be seen, most of the original manuscripts still reside with Lady Bliss in London. It is expected that, after her death, the provenance will be Cambridge University Library;

(3)  a selected <u>discography</u> of commercially produced long-playing records. Each recording is listed alphabetically by title, and each work prefaced by a mnemonic "D." Reference is made to reviews of the recordings cited in the "Bibliography" and,

(4)  an annotated <u>bibliography</u> of writings by and about Arthur Bliss, his style and his music, with annotations often taking the form of quotations taken from reviews. Each citation is preceded by the mnemonic "B." Entries in the Bibliography refer to the "Works and Performances" and "Discography" sections.

In addition, appendices provide alphabetical and chronological listings of Bliss's works. A complete general <u>index</u> of names (personal and corporate) concludes the volume.

# Acknowledgments

This volume is dedicated to Lady Bliss, who helped in so many ways and who welcomed me into her house so many times while I consulted the many papers and manuscripts that were at that time kept under her roof. Thanks to the unfailing warmth of her welcome, my task was made a delight to me. I must also thank my wife, Valerie, and children for their unfailing support.

Many other people helped me in a number of ways, in particular : Dr. W.R. Aitken; Elizabeth H. Auman of the Library of Congress; the late Bernard Axcell; Lt. Col. Rodney Bashford; the late Sir Adrian Boult; Mrs. C. Brown of the B.B.C. Written Archives Centre; H.J. Brown; J.E. Brown (Lehigh University Band); the late George H.W. Budge; H.M. Butler; Professor Frank Callaway; George Dannatt; the late Professor Thorold Dickinson; the late Dr. Vincent Duckles; Winifred Ferrier; Mrs. Julian F. Forbes; Dr. Watson Forbes; Sir Denis Forman of GRANADA TV; Peter Racine Fricker; Sir Charles Groves; the Rt. Hon. Edward Heath; Sir Gilbert Inglefield; Miss Muriel James; Michael Kennedy; Jane Lea; Professor Denis McCaldin; the late Sir William McKie; the Rt. Rev. Michael Mann, Dean of Windsor; Harry Mortimer; Lord Olivier; the late Elizabeth Poston; the late J.B. Priestley; Lionel Salter; John Sanders; Arthur Searle of the British Library; Miss Phyllis Sellick; Wayne Shirley of the Library of Congress; Miss Rosamund Strode of the Britten-Pears Library; L.G. Tagg; Sir John Tooley; Dame Ninette de Valois; Mrs. Ursula Vaughan Williams; the late Sir William Walton and Lady Walton; Sir David Willcocks; Derek Williams of Cambridge University Library; Paul S. Wilson; Miss Margueritte Wolff and Nicholas Wooler.

I must also record my thanks to Mrs. Helen Crute and Mrs. Janet Johnson of The Secretariat for translating my unintelligible scrawl into a magnificently typed script.

# Arthur Bliss

# Biography

Arthur Edward Drummond Bliss was born in London on 2 August 1891. His father, Francis E. Bliss, a native of Springfield, Massachusetts, had come to England as Chairman of the Anglo-American Oil Company in 1888. His mother, who married Francis Bliss in 1890, was English and a talented pianist; she died, tragically young, in 1895. Francis Bliss retired from business in 1900 but remained in England and brought up his family in London.

There were two other sons of the marriage: Francis Kennard Bliss, born in 1892 and Howard James, born in 1894. All three brothers were gifted musicians: Arthur was a pianist, Kennard played the clarinet and Howard the 'cello. Through the help and encouragement of their father, music played a large part in their childhood, both at home and in their two schools. At a concert at Bilton Grange in 1904, "...A.E.D. Bliss's playing is excellent. The accuracy and brilliance of his runs shows assiduous and careful practice.... The 'cello solo by J.H. Bliss (a prospective member of the school) calls for special mention. The performer, who is not yet ten years of age, played a most difficult piece with unusual facility in one so young, and will be a great musical acquisition to the school when he joins us next term."(1) From Bilton Grange the boys went on to Rugby School and from there Bliss entered Pembroke College, Cambridge, where he studied Music with Charles Wood and graduated in 1913 with a B.A. in History and a Mus.Bac. It was at Cambridge that Vaughan Williams made a great impression on Bliss, both as a musician and as a man; later they were to become firm friends. At Cambridge he also met E.J. Dent through whom, in later years, Bliss was to find the stimulus of contemporary music on the Continent.

Then followed nearly a year at the Royal College of Music in London, studying composition with Charles Villiers Stanford; the Director of the College at that time was Sir Hubert Parry. Contemporary students were Herbert Howells, Eugene Goossens and Arthur Benjamin; with them Bliss relished performances of opera and ballet. "These evenings were shot through with unexpected excitements, as the curtain went up on a Bakst design or the opening notes of a Stravinsky score were heard. On a return home from such a feast, we seemed to board the bus with the dash of a Nijinsky leap."(2)

In August 1914, a week after the declaration of war and two weeks after his twenty-third birthday, Bliss enlisted and after a few weeks' training became a Second Lieutenant in the 13th Royal Fusiliers. He fought in France, being mentioned in despatches, until he was wounded at the Battle of the Somme in July 1916. His brother Kennard, fighting only a few miles ways, was killed at Thiepval in September, eight days after his twenty-first birthday. Writing of his brother's death to Dent, Bliss said: "...Kennard was killed instantly and was spared any pain. I almost feel glad that a person such as he was spared a longer existence in such awful surroundings."(3) Bliss recovered from his wound and, after serving as an instructor at a cadet school in England for a few months, returned to France as a Captain in the Grenadier Guards. He was gassed at Cambrai in 1918.

Throughout the grim conditions of the trenches Bliss maintained a determined connection with the world of music. He was helped in this by a flow of gramophone records sent by his father; correspondence with Parry and other friends; a visit on leave to Elgar who sent him a miniature score of Cockaigne with "Good Luck" inscribed on the cover, and even performances of his works in London, although he was not there to hear them.

In January 1919, a week after demobilisation from the Army, Bliss was back at the Royal College of Music. In a broadcast interview, Bliss said of this time in his life, "...I suddenly felt that I'd come together as a personality and I felt that my technical equipment was behindhand, and I sat down to work with feverish activity.... I copied out a whole act of Figaro in order to find out about this beautiful, limpid scoring. I worked every day at something connected with my art. I went and spent a good deal of time trying to find out what other people were doing; I went over to Paris and met all the remarkable group there... men like Picasso and Cocteau and Poulenc, Milhaud, Honegger - it was a most extraordinary interesting time... the whole thing seemed to me a wonderfully explosive force for any young man starting off. And, as I say, I felt my ability, my technical ability, had been so frustrated and delayed by the war that I had to put in double time."(4)

Very soon he became a notable figure in the post-war world. Conducting engagements were many and various: Bach, Pergolesi, Berlioz, Holst, Vaughan Williams and Stravinsky - a comprehensive repertoire. He remained an excellent conductor for the rest of his life; orchestras, choirs, brass bands all respected him and enjoyed playing under him.

With his compositions he quickly made a reputation as an innovator, exhibiting a deliberate astringency which both shocked and delighted his audiences. All were chamber works but all revealed a vigorous personality, an adventurer making important explorations in sound. Rout and Rhapsody used the voice as part of an orchestral combination; in Rout the soprano sings a medley of made-up syllables, and in <u>Rhapsody</u> the mezzo-soprano and the tenor vocalise on 'ah'.

In later years Bliss was unfailingly generous and helpful to young composers, both personally and through the various official posts he held.  Looking back at his own adventurous youth he said, "...everyone at twenty should be Athenian-minded.  He should think that the new is all-important.  He should believe that it <u>must</u> be new to be good, and if it <u>is</u> new, it <u>is</u> good.  But at 45, one should not be so shuttle-minded, one should have sifted much of the new into two distinct groups; that which is a mere fashion which dies with next year's models, and that very small, scarce and seemingly permanent fraction which enriches one's own art."(5)

The first major orchestral work, <u>A Colour Symphony</u>, owes its existence to Elgar at whose suggestion it was commissioned by the Three Choirs Festival and given its first performance at Gloucester in September 1922, the composer conducting.  Then it provoked dislike and ridicule as well as interest and admiration; but after a triumphant London performance in the following March, Bliss's reputation as a force in English music was established.  At this time Bliss's father, now 76, decided to spend his remaining years in the land of his birth, and in April 1923 sailed with his family for New York. Francis Bliss had married in 1918 a widow with two children and there was a little daughter of this marriage.  It was for these children, Cynthia, Patrick and Enid, that Bliss set three poems by Walter de la Mare, <u>Three Romantic Songs</u>, which had their first performance in London in 1922.  So the family that crossed the Atlantic was considerable.  Once in America, Bliss flung himself into the new world with his characteristic zest.  He accompanied his father to California but returned to the East in time for the Pittfield Festival in September where began for him the friendship with Elizabeth Sprague Coolidge, from whose generosity and enthusiasm composers such as Bridge, Malipiero, Schoenberg, Bliss and others were to benefit.  The next few months were spent in the stimulating atmosphere of New York: here he wrote another voice and chamber ensemble work, but this time with real words, a setting of poems by the Chinese poet Li Po.  By January 1924 he had rejoined his father who was now settled in Santa Barbara.  Never inactive musically, Bliss was soon conducting in the Hollywood Bowl, playing in a chamber ensemble, writing music criticisms and composing songs and piano works, and in Santa Barbara he met and married his wife.  Known to her friends as Trudy, Gertrude Hoffmann was the daughter of a distinguished American naturalist; thus a further transatlantic and very important element was added to Bliss's life.  They were married in June of the following year and then, despite Bliss's affection for America, feeling that his "future inevitably lay in England," he returned with his wife to London.(6)

America had made its mark and both the next two important works were written with the precision and vitality of the great American orchestras in his mind.  <u>Introduction and Allegro</u>, 1926, is dedicated to Leopold Stokowski and the Philadelphia Orchestra, who gave the first performance of it in America.  Pierre Monteux, who had already performed <u>A</u>

Colour Symphony in Boston, gave the first performance of Hymn to Apollo with the Concertgebouw Orchestra in Amsterdam.  In both works the earlier influence of Stravinsky and Les Six has dwindled, and the brilliant Bliss of the jeux d'esprit has developed an orchestral language of his own.  Bliss revised both these works in later years, and also revised A Colour Symphony only ten years after it had been written; revision was a habit with him for all his life.

The achievements of the years after his return to England were prodigious.  Not for Bliss the frivolity of the Twenties, nor the emotional self-destruction of the Thirties. Happy in his marriage and a growing family, with a settled place of his own in which to work, Bliss was conscious not only of the lost five years of the War but of his great good fortune in having survived.  Still the explorer and now with great technical assurance, he set to work.

First came a commission from Mrs. Coolidge, the Oboe Quintet written for her concert in Venice in September 1927.  Next, Pastoral: Lie Strewn the White Flocks in which Bliss used, for the first time, the anthology form he was to adopt in his later choral works; words chosen from poets of different centuries, different countries, but expressing a similarity of theme.  Bliss wrote of this work: "Elgar, whose music I had loved ever since I sang, as a boy in his Dream of Gerontius, gave me permission to dedicate Pastoral to him. In the introduction of the last section listeners will note my adoption of the characteristic drooping sevenths, perhaps the sincerest way to show my debt to him."(7)  In the same year he wrote Serenade for baritone and orchestra, again using the words of different poets.  This work Bliss dedicated to his wife.

The choral symphony, Morning Heroes, a major work, was a requiem for those killed in World War I.  Again the anthology form and again an innovation, for in this work the soloist is not a singer but an orator.  "The orator has a very impressive part.  It is he who deals with the whole episode of Hector's farewell accompanied by the orchestra, and at the end he declaims 'a Spring Offensive' to the accompaniment of drums alone.  The story opens with his words 'So Andromache met Hector now ....' and his last line 'Why speak they not of comrades that went under', is the unanswerable final word of the argument."(8)  The music critic of The Times wrote "... we realise that Arthur Bliss has made a great step forward, and in saying what is old, he has said something new and true."(9)

The Clarinet Quintet, written for Frederick Thurston, and the lesser known Viola Sonata, written for Lionel Tertis, appeared in the early 1930's.  Then in 1934, Bliss broke entirely new ground by writing the film score for Alexander Korda's production of Things to Come, based on the novel by H.G. Wells.  New ground for Bliss and new ground for the film world of the mid-thirties, for music was to be part of the constructive theme of the film: Wells said "Bliss is to be a collaborator in its production.  In this, as in so many respects, this film is to be boldly experimental.  The Bliss music is not intended to be tacked on, it is part of the

design"(10).  The orchestral suite that Bliss subsequently
arranged from this film music has always been very popular.
Things to Come was the first of eight films for which Bliss
was to write the music.  Among them are Men of Two Worlds
(titled Kisenga, Man of Africa in America) 1945, Seven Waves
Away (titled Abandon Ship in America) 1945, Christopher
Columbus 1949 and The Beggar's Opera with Laurence Olivier,
directed by Peter Brook, in 1952-3.

To clear his mind from the turbulent task of collaborating
with Korda and Wells, Bliss wrote Music for Strings.  This
music originates from the English tradition of Purcell,
Tallis, Vaughan Williams and Elgar; but from the exhilarating
leap of the opening phrase to the last note of the final
Presto the writing is unmistakably Arthur Bliss.  After so
abstract a work as Music for Strings, which had no literary
or visual stimulus involved in its inception, Bliss went on
to a work with a dramatic plot and immense visual impact, his
first ballet, Checkmate.  Bliss had already arranged and
composed incidental music for the stage: As You Like It,
1919; The Tempest, 1921; King Solomon, 1924.  He had known
and admired Diaghilev and had worked with Ninette de Valois
in 1927.  Checkmate was commissioned by the Sadler's Wells
Ballet Company for their first visit to Paris and was
performed there in June 1937.  In the choreography de Valois,
like Wells in Things to Come, is stating clearly the menace
of the coming European war.  The sets and costumes were by
the American artist McKnight Kauffer, and very much of the
period.  It is interesting to note that for the section Dance
of the Castles,  Bliss used the music he had written for the
Machine Sequence in Things to Come, and just as he had made a
very successful suite from the film music, so the orchestral
suite of Dances from Checkmate is very popular.

Kenilworth, 1937 was also a commission, Bliss having been
asked to write the test piece for the annual Brass Band
Championship.  Thirty-six years later he was again asked to
write the Champion test piece, and for this he wrote The
Belmont Variations, Belmont being the town near Boston where
Bliss's wife was born.

It should be noted here that from 1935 onwards (the year of
Things to Come) the majority of Bliss's works were written in
response to commissions or requests.  He himself commented on
this, "I know ... that I have great difficulty in starting a
work unless stirred by some dramatic intention.  I do not
mean so realistic an urge as a libretto or scenario, but that
I have to wait patiently until some phrase or rhythm or
series of sounds leaps into my mind (much as an actor comes
onto the stage) to foreshadow for me musical action and
development.  Once I have that dramatic entry I can write
with facility.  It has therefore been fortunate for me that
most of my works have been demanded for definite occasions.
The thought of a particular player or a group of singers and
especially of the mise en scene has been sufficient to set me
writing."(11)

The next commission, to write a piano concerto for the
British Week in the New York World's Fair, provided all and
more than he could wish for as a 'dramatic entry'.  The mise

en scene New York, the players Solomon and the New York
Philharmonic Orchestra, the conductor his great friend and
colleague, Adrian Boult. Here was a chance to reaffirm his
affection for America; the writing of it gave him great
pleasure and the dedication is 'To the People of the United
States of America'.

Thus June 1939 found Bliss in New York; with him were his
wife and two daughters. They spent the summer visiting
American relatives in New England and were on their way to
Quebec, from where they were to sail for England, when war
was declared. In As I Remember, Bliss describes the
situation: "A week of desperate indecision followed. What
should I try to do, with my wife still holding her American
passport, and with my daughters aged 13 and 7? At first we
attempted to get passage on a later ship from Canada, and
then the news of the sinking of a non-combatant ship made it
seem madness to risk their lives. Adrian was already back in
England, and I cabled him to find out whether I myself could
be of any practical use if I returned. His advice was to
wait, and in this interim of doubt I accepted the invitation
proffered me from the University of California."(12) Bliss
and his family then travelled to Berkeley and he took up the
post of Visiting Professor of Music in January 1940. Bliss
remained in Berkeley until the spring of 1941 when, at the
request of the BBC, he returned to take up the post of
Assistant Director of Overseas Music. Later in 1942 he was
made Director of Music. Two of his main achievements during
the years at the BBC were (a) his music statement of Music
Policy which laid the foundation for the Third Programme, now
Radio 3, and (b) his successful championship of British
composers.(13) In 1943 his family was at last able to rejoin
him in London. There are three works which give ample
evidence of the effect the second war had on Bliss's
emotional life. Outwardly he was cheerful and optimistic;
his letters to his wife were full of hope and comfort, his
work at the BBC was efficient and characteristically
innovative, and the administrative ability inherited from his
father was plain to see. But Seven American Poems, written
in 1940 (settings of words by Elinor Wylie and Edna St.
Vincent Millay) express lost happiness; the Quartet
commissioned by Mrs. Coolidge, written painfully in the
winter of 1940-41, is brittle and bitter; while the ballet,
Miracle in the Gorbals, written in 1944, has as its theme
tenderness and compassion destroyed by brutality; the slash
of the open razors is far more explicit than the stylised
death of the Red King.

Bliss's next ballet Adam Zero is perhaps not as well known as
Checkmate: it contains a stunning night-club scene which,
with its brilliant use of syncopated rhythms reflects the
influence of contemporary jazz on him as on other composers
of the period. This ballet was staged soon after the Royal
Ballet's accession to Covent Garden in 1946, and was regarded
by Bliss as his best. The Lady of Shalott, Bliss's fourth
ballet, written in 1957, was commissioned by the University
of California at Berkeley for the dedication of the Albert
Hertz Memorial Hall of Music during the May T.Morrison Music
Festival in 1958. Here again is a continuation of the

American connection and a renewal of his special relationship
with the University of California.

In 1934 Bliss and his wife had acquired a few acres of
woodland a hundred miles west of London, and had a holiday
house built and designed on very modern lines by P.J.B.
Harland.  There was a small music room quite separate from
the house itself, in which many of the works Bliss wrote in
the thirties had been composed.  In 1944 they made Pen Pits,
as it was called, their home the year round, and it was there
that Bliss's opera The Olympians was written; the libretto
was by his great friend, J.B. Priestley.

Bliss described The Olympians as a 'Romantic Opera with a
Touch of Terror.'  The production, handicapped by lack of
rehearsal and by an inexperienced opera company, had only a
moderate success.  In a long letter of comfort and
encouragement Dent wrote: "... I have now seen your opera
three times, and I can honestly say that I have enjoyed it
more and more each time.... Our critics are complete fools
and lamentably ignorant when they write about any sort of
opera; I have spent my life in trying to teach them
something, but they are hopeless, I fear."  He also deplored
the inadequacy of the cast and the production and ends,"...it
is indispensable that you should go on writing
operas...."(14)

Bliss's second opera, Tobias and the Angel, was one of the
first to be written for television and was successfully
performed in May 1960.

In the Autumn of 1953 Bliss was appointed Master of the
Queen's Music.  His sense of history, his sense of the
dramatic and his professional expertise all fitted him for
the task of creating ceremonial music for state occasions.
Most of these would be heard in splendid settings: an example
is a work written for the service to commemorate the nine
hundredth anniversary of Westminster Abbey; Ceremonial
Prelude is the majestic music that accompanied the Queen's
procession from the West door of the Abbey to the Shrine of
St.Edward the Confessor, where Her Majesty laid a tribute of
red roses.  Equally appropriate are the small-scale settings
for unaccompanied voices of poems by C.Day Lewis and Eric
Crozier:  these were broadcast at the birth of the younger
Princes.  Bliss enjoyed solving the problems presented by
these 'occasional pieces', and many of them continue in
concert performances today.  Bliss was conscientious in
discharging all the duties of the appointment and, as a
public musical figure holding an official post, he felt a
responsibility for British musicians and for British music.
He was, for example, in the forefront of the Performing Right
Society's fight in 1955-56 over certain provisions of the
Copyright Bill (then going through Parliament) which it was
felt would destroy a large part of English musical life and
jeopardise the livelihood of composers and authors.  But this
was nothing new; he had taken an active part in the musical
world since 1919.  He wrote and spoke well, as the
bibliography shows; there are articles by him in musical
journals from 1919 onwards: he had lectured on Modern Music
to the Royal Institution in 1934, and in 1935 he broadcast

the introduction to the first of the BBC Symphony concerts. Time spent in committee, in correspondence (letters were meticulously answered in his own hand) and in travelling abroad on behalf of British music was generously given.  But his championship was not only for music; for many years he also took an active interest in children and their welfare. An example is the letters he wrote to <u>The Times</u>, and to the Secretary of State for Health, about the neglected child, Maria Colwell, and the boy left by his mother to starve to death. (15)

Among the many positions he held were: Chairman of the Music Committee of the British Council, President of the Performing Right Society and President of the Composers' Guild.  In 1956 he led a group of musicians to Russia, giving concerts in Leningrad, Moscow, Kiev and Kharkov, and two years later he returned to Moscow as a member of the Jury of the Tchaikowsky International Competition for pianists.  In 1964, he travelled in Japan with the London Symphony Orchestra (of which he was Honorary President from 1956 until his death), conducting his <u>Colour Symphony</u> and <u>Dances from Checkmate</u>.

But here it must be emphasised that the public figure and the composer were two distinct entities.  Near the end of his life, Bliss himself was outspoken on this point.  In a revealing analysis of a work (16) written nearly twenty years earlier he declared that this duality would not be apparent except to the discerning, that only in his music would be found his real, his private personality.(17)

In 1954 Pen Pits was too remote to be practical so Bliss and his wife moved back to a quiet corner of London and here he lived until his death, and here were written the works in the last twenty years of his life.  They were many and various: the <u>Violin Concerto</u> had already been commissioned, and two movements of it written at the time of the appointment of Master of the Queen's Music, but was interrupted for two years by official and public duties.  <u>The Beatitudes</u>, the large scale choral work which was commissioned for the 1962 opening of the new Cathedral at Coventry, was the occasion of one of the great disappointments in Bliss's musical career. He had understood that the performance was to have been in the Cathedral, using the magnificent organ, but only a month before the concert, Bliss was told that the performance would be in a cinema, with a small electronic organ.  Bliss, with characteristic courtesy, accepted the decision without protest; it is ironic that the last major choral work, in which the organ also has an important role, was never heard by him.  The librettist of <u>The Beatitudes</u> was Christopher Hassall who also wrote the texts of <u>Tobias and the Angel</u> and <u>Mary of Magdala</u>.  There was great friendship between the two men, and the harmonious collaboration was halted only by Hassall's untimely death in 1963.

Previous to these choral works were the <u>Sonata for Piano</u> and the <u>Quartet</u> composed for the Griller Quartet, a virtuoso piece of which Sidney Griller made frequent use when teaching during his many years at the Royal Academy of Music. Concurrently with all these major works were anthems, fanfares, songs written for children and the music requested for various state occasions.

In 1966 he began his autobiography, <u>As I Remember</u>, which was published by Faber & Faber in 1970.  In this Bliss gives an excellent account of his life and activities, but, except for the letters written to his wife and two daughters during the Second World War, intimacy is characteristically withheld.

But about the principles of his craft Bliss was always articulate.  He liked the image used by T.E. Hulme in describing the tension proper to a successful work of art. In Bliss's words "... composition can be compared to the bending of an intractable and springy piece of steel into the exact shape which you intend it to have".(18)"... composition is compelling it by the grip of the fingers and the weight of the body to take up against its will the exact position and shapes demanded...  I believe that the emotion resulting from apprehended beauty should be solidified and fixed by presenting it in a form absolutely fitting to it and to it alone.  If I were to define my musical goal it would be to try for an emotion truly felt and caught forever in a formal perfection."(19)

How close did Bliss come to his goal? "... it will be a fascinating exercise for future musical historians to assess not only the liberating influence that Bliss, the young explorer of new sounds had in the early Twenties, but also the steadying influence that he exerted in his later years as England's senior composer."(20)

In 1969 an invitation came from the Aldeburgh Festival: there was to be a concert of music of any century written by composers when they were very young or when very old. Bliss's contribution was <u>The World is Charged with the Grandeur of God</u>, scored for mixed chorus, 2 flutes, 3 trumpets and 4 trombones; the text is by Gerard Manley Hopkins.  Here is Bliss, 'the explorer of new sounds' indeed! And here is the first of those works written in the last five years of his life, which were informed again by the fire and intensity of his youth, and shaped with the mastery acquired through the intervening years.  Next came the <u>Cello Concerto</u> (1970), written at the request of Rostropovitch; a welcome invitation for, just as the first work that Bliss had written for the clarinet was the <u>Rhapsody No.1</u> (now lost), which Kennard first performed at a concert in Cambridge in 1914, so he had always wanted to write a work for 'cello and orchestra ever since, as a young man, he had played through the classical repertoire with Howard, the brilliant 'cellist of the boyhood trios and duets.

In 1972 there followed a large-scale set of variations for orchestra: its title is <u>Metamorphic Variations</u> because Bliss claimed "... the three themes that constitute the opening section called 'Elements', undergo a greater transformation than the simple word Variation implies". (21)

One of the works written at the very end of his life gave Bliss great pleasure: <u>Spirit of the Age</u> was a commission from the BBC to write the prelude and postlude over the titles of a television series that explored, with great distinction, eight centuries of British architecture. Bliss was frail by then but he was well enough to conduct the pre-recording himself. The work is scored for brass and percussion and the players were old friends and colleagues from the London Symphony Orchestra.

The last major work, Shield of Faith, was a commission to write a choral work for the quincentenary of St. George's Chapel, Windsor in 1975. The text consists of five poems ranging over the five centuries since the foundation of the Chapel; once again and for the last time, the anthology form. In this felicitous work his own apprehension of beauty and the creation of ceremonial music were perfectly fused. He saw the work in print but did not live to be present at the occasion for which it had been written. It is 'Dedicated by Gracious Permission to Her Majesty Queen Elizabeth II'.

Arthur Bliss died on 27th March 1975. He had been Master of the Queen's Music for twenty-two years. He was knighted in 1950, made Knight Commander of the Victorian Order in 1969 and Companion of Honour in 1971. On 20th May, a Service of Thanksgiving for his life and work was held in Westminster Abbey; his own anthem Sing Mortals was finely sung and at the conclusion of the Service, before the pealing of the Abbey bells there rang out, superbly performed, Fanfare for Heroes.

1.  Extract from The Bilton Record, June 1904, p.113
2.  Arthur Bliss, As I Remember (1970) p.28
3.  Undated letter from Bliss to Dent (CUL Add. 7973)
4.  From Personal Call No.63 (BBC) : London Calling Asia, 30 May 1955
5.  Arthur Bliss : First lecture to the Royal Institution, 8 March 1934
6.  Arthur Bliss, As I Remember (1970) p.84
7.  Programme note by the composer : Henry Wood Promenade Concert, 26 August 1960.
8.  Scott Goddard on Morning Heroes in Radio Times, 17 March 1939, p.14
9.  Report in The Times, 24 October 1930, p.12
10. Bliss quoting H.G. Wells in an interview with Muir Mathieson, 11 April 1974 (GRANADA TV Historical Record)
11. Arthur Bliss, Self Portrait in a Performing Right Society concert programme, Royal Festival Hall, 26 January 1955
12. Arthur Bliss, As I Remember (1970) p.122
13. See Nicholas Kenyon, The BBC Symphony Orchestra : the first 50 years 1930-1980 (BBC, 1981), pp.172-187, for full details
14. Letter from Dent to Bliss, 3 November 1949 (Lady Bliss)
15. See B127 and B198 for details
16. Meditations on a theme by John Blow (1955)
17. GRANADA TV interview ( 1974)
18. Arthur Bliss : First lecture to the Royal Institution, 8 March 1934
19. Arthur Bliss : Third lecture to the Royal Institution, 22 March 1934
20. David Willcocks's address at the Memorial Service, Westminster Abbey, 20 May 1975
21. Programme notes by the composer (1973)

# Works and Performances

"See" references, e.g., <u>See</u> : B173, identify citations
in the "Bibliography" section.

I.    OPERAS

W1.   <u>LA SERVA PADRONA</u> (1918-19; unpublished) <u>See</u> : B381

        Opera by Pergolesi (1710-1736), arranged by
        Bliss.  Three  singers  and  chamber  ensemble.
        Unable  to  trace  instrumentation.  Libretto
        translated by Grace Lovat Fraser. Location of
        manuscript : unable to trace

        <u>Premier</u>

W1a.  1919 (29 January) : Hammersmith (London); the
        Lyric  Opera  House;  Uberto : John  Barclay;
        Vespone: Tom Reynolds; Serpina : Grace Crawford;
        Mr.  Albert  Fox's  sextet;  C.Lovat  Fraser,
        scenery; Nigel Playfair, producer. <u>See</u> : B39

W2.   <u>THE OLYMPIANS</u> (1945-49; Novello; 147 min.) <u>See</u>:B387

        Opera in three acts.
        11 singers/chorus/ballet of girls /2+2.2.2.2+1/
        4.2.3.1/timp/perc(3)cel/2hps (unis)/strings (+6
        off-stage tpts in 2 parts)
        Libretto by J.B. Priestley
        Dedicated to my friend and colleague of many
        years, Harold Brooke
        Location  of  manuscript:University  Library,
        Cambridge

        <u>Premier</u>

W2a.  1949 (29 September): London; Royal Opera House,
        Covent Garden; The Cure: Murray Dickie; Madame
        Bardeau:  Edith  Coates;  Jean:  Ronald  Lewis;
        Joseph Lavatte: Howell Glynne; Hector de Florac:
        James Johnston; Madeleine: Shirley Russell;

Alfred: Rhydderch Davies; Mercury: Robert Helpmann; Venus: Moyra Fraser; Bacchus: Thorsteinn Hannesson; Mars: David Franklin; Diana: Margherita Grandi; Jupiter: Kenneth Schon; Covent Garden Opera Chorus; Sadler's Wells School Corps de Ballet; Covent Garden Orchestra; Karl Rankl, conductor; John Bryan, scenery and costumes; Pauline Grant, choreography; Peter Brook, producer. See : B62,B63,B258,B348,B370,B371

## Other selected performances

W2b.  1972 (21 February): London; Royal Festival Hall; The Cure: Bernard Dickerson; Madame Bardeau: Shirley Minty; Joseph Lavatte: Forbes Robinson; Hector de Florac: William McAlpine; Madeleine: Anne Pashley; Mercury: silent part; Venus: silent part; Bacchus: Edmund Bohan; Mars: Raimund Herincx; Diana: Rae Woodland; Jupiter: Thomas Hemsley; The Ambrosian Singers; Polyphonia Orchestra; Bryan Fairfax: conductor; Ande Anderson: producer. See : B410,B448

W3.  TOBIAS AND THE ANGEL (1958-9; Novello; 95 min.) See: B297

Opera in two acts
10 singers/chorus/2+1.2.2.2/4.2.3.1/timp/perc(2) /hp/strings
Libretto by Christopher Hassall after The Book of Tobit
Commissioned by BBC Television
Dedicated to Trudy Bliss by the composer and the author
Location of manuscript: Lady Bliss, London

## Premier

W3a.  1960 (19 May): London; BBC Television Centre; Bozru: Trevor Anthony; Rhezia: Carolyn Maia; Tobias: John Ford; Azarias: Ronald Lewis; Tobit: Jess Walters; Anna: Janet Howe; Raquel: Richard Golding; Sara: Elaine Malbin; Asmoday: Roy Patrick; Beggar: William Lyon Brown; London Symphony Orchestra; Norman del Mar, conductor; Margaret Dale, choreographer; Maureen Heneghan, wardrobe; Clifford Hatts, designer; Rudolf Cartier, producer. See : B442

II.  BALLETS

W4.  ADAM ZERO (1946; Novello; 40 min.) See:B303,B345

Ballet in one scene for full orchestra
2+2.2+1.2(+ten. sax. ad lib).2/4.2.3.1/timp/perc (4)/cel/hp/strings
Scenario by Michael Benthall
Dedicated to Constant Lambert

Location of manuscript : University Library, Cambridge

Premiere

W4a.  1946 (10 April): London; Royal Opera House, Covent Garden; Sadler's Wells Ballet; Constant Lambert, conductor; Robert Helpmann, choreography; Roger Furse, scenery and costumes. See : B25

Other selected performances

W4b.  1946 (16 September): London; Royal Albert Hall; BBC Symphony Orchestra; Constant Lambert, conductor (Orchestral Suite). See: B317

W4c.  1966 (13 May): Macclesfield; Assembly Hall of the King's School; BBC Northern Orchestra; Arthur Bliss, conductor (Fanfare Prelude). See: B103

W4d.  1970 (9 December): London; Emma Cons Hall (Morley College); Cyril Smith & Phyllis Sellick, pianos (Fun and Games for Phyllis and Cyril)

W5.   CHECKMATE (1937; Novello; 45-50 min.) See:B20,B105, B133,B199,B243,B303,B329

Ballet in one scene with prologue for full orchestra 2.1+1.1.1/4.3.3.0/timp/perc(2)/hp/ strings
Scenario by Arthur Bliss
Dedicated to R.O. Morris
Location of manuscript : The British Library, London

Premier

W5a.  1937 (15 June): Paris; Theatre des Champs - Elysees; Vic - Wells Ballet; Constant Lambert, conductor; Ninette de Valois, choreography; E. McKnight Kauffer, scenery and costumes. See: B1

Other selected performances

W5b.  1937 (5 October): London; Sadler's Wells Theatre; Vic - Wells Ballet; Constant Lambert, conductor. See:B80

W5c.  1938 (7 April): London; Queen's Hall; London Philharmonic Orchestra; Arthur Bliss, conductor (Concert Suite). See:B347

W5d.  1939 (16 November): New York; Carnegie Hall; New York Philharmonic - Symphony Orchestra; Arthur Bliss, conductor (Concert Suite). See: B240

W6.   THE FESTIVAL OF FLORA (1927; unpublished)

Masque ballet with music by Henry Purcell (1659-1695), arranged by Arthur Bliss and Cyril Bradley Rootham

Chorus and ensemble. Unable to trace instrumentation
Scenario after Hortensie Mancini, Duchesse de Mazarin. Location of manuscript: unable to trace

Premiere

W6a.   1927 (31 May): London; New Scala Theatre; Teatro Della Piccole Maschere; Leigh Henry, musical director.

W7.    THE LADY OF SHALOTT (1957-8; unpublished but handled by Novello; 35-40 min.) See : B17

Ballet in one act for full orchestra
2+1.2.2.2/   2.2.1.0/   timp/perc(1)/cel/pno/hp/ strings
Scenario by Arthur Bliss and Christopher Hassall based on the poem by Alfred, Lord Tennyson (1809-1892)
Commissioned by the University of California for the May T. Morrison Music Festival
Location of manuscript : Lady Bliss, London

Premiere

W7a.   1958 (2 May): University of California (Berkeley Campus); Alfred Hertz Memorial Hall of Music; San Francisco Ballet; Earl Murray, conductor; Lew Christensen, choreography; Tony Duquette, scenary and costumes. See: B261

Other selected performances

W7b.   1975 (13 May): Leicester; Haymarket Theatre; New Park Girls' School Ballet Group; Eric Pinkett, conductor; Mary Hockney, choreography; M.J. Laxton, scenery; J. Hammond, costumes. See: B147

W7c.   1968 (30 December): London; BBC Maida Vale Studio 1; BBC Symphony Orchestra; Arthur Bliss, conductor (Orchestral Suite). See: B379, B380

W8.    MIRACLE IN THE GORBALS (1944; Novello; 35 min.) See: B107,B243,B256,B297,B303,B400

Ballet in one scene for full orchestra
2+1.2+1.2+1.2/4.2.3.0/ timp/perc (1)/hp/strings
Scenario by Michael Benthall
Dedicated to Trudy, Barbara, Karan - thanks- giving for 5 November 1943
Location of manuscript: Lady Bliss, London

Premiere

W8a.   1944 (26 October): London; Prince's Theatre; Sadler's Wells Ballet; Constant Lambert, conductor; Robert Helpmann, choreography; Edward Burra, scenery; Grace Kelly, costumes. See: B82

Other selected performances

W8b.   1945  (15  June):  Cheltenham;  Town  Hall;  London
       Philharmonic Orchestra; Arthur Bliss, conductor
       (Concert Suite).

## III. ORCHESTRAL MUSIC

W9.    A BIRTHDAY GREETING TO HER MAJESTY, 21 APRIL 1955
       ON THE REFRAIN : HAPPY BIRTHDAY TO YOU, OUR QUEEN
       ELIZABETH   (1955; unpublished; 1 minute 42 secs)

       2.2+1.2.2/4.3.3.1/timp/perc (3)/hp/org/strings
       Location of manuscript: Lady Bliss, London

Premiere

W9a.   1955  (21  April):  London;  Royal  Festival  Hall;
       National  Youth  Orchestra  of  Great  Britain;
       Malcolm Sargent, conductor.  See: B29

W10.   A COLOUR SYMPHONY (1921-22; Curwen/Boosey & Hawkes;
       30 min.) See: B267,B334,B356,B369,B427,B428

       3+3.3+1.3+1.3+1/4.3.3.1/timp/perc  (3)/hp  (2)/
       strings.  Commissioned by the 1922 Three Choirs
       Festival.
       Dedicated to Adrian Boult
       Location of manuscripts: Music Division, Library
       of Congress (original)  - first movement only;
       unable to trace (revised)

Premieres

W10a.  1922 (September): Gloucester; Cathedral Church of
       the  Holy  Trinity;  London  Symphony  Orchestra;
       Arthur Bliss, conductor. See: B94,B95,B328,B412

W10b.  1923 (10 March): London; Queen's Hall; New Queen's
       Hall  Orchestra;  Arthur  Bliss,  conductor.  See:
       B14,B425

W10c.  1924 (5 January): New York; Carnegie Hall; Boston
       Symphony Orchestra; Pierre Monteux, conductor.
       See: B241

Other selected performances

W10d.  1928 (4 October): London; Queen's Hall; Henry J.
       Wood Symphony Orchestra; Arthur Bliss, conductor
       (Pyanepsion).  See: B70, B456

W10e.  1932  (27  April):  London;  Queen's  Hall;  BBC
       Symphony  Orchestra;  Adrian  Boult,  conductor
       (Revised version).  See: B72,B312,B431

W11.   CONCERTO  FOR  PIANO  AND  ORCHESTRA  IN  B-FLAT
       (1938-39; Novello; 38 min.)  See: B269

       2+1.2.2.2/4.2.3.0./timp/strings

Commissioned by The British Council for the
British Week at the New York World Fair, 1939
Dedicated to the People of the United States of
America
Location of manuscript: Royal College of Music,
London

## Premieres

W11a. 1939 (10 June): New York; Carnegie Hall; Solomon,
piano; New York Philharmonic Symphony Orchestra;
Adrian Boult, conductor. See: B242

W11b. 1939 (17 August): London; Queen's Hall; Solomon,
piano; London Symphony Orchestra; Henry J. Wood,
conductor. See: B66, B349

W12. CONCERTO FOR PIANO, TENOR VOICE, STRINGS AND
PERCUSSION (1921; Oxford University Press; 12 min.)
See: B210

Location of manuscript: unable to trace

## Premiere

W12a. 1921 (11 June): London; Wigmore Hall; Myra Hess,
piano; Steuart Wilson, tenor; special orchestra;
Arthur Bliss, conductor. See: B19,B83,B413,B432

## Other selected performances

W12b. 1924 (19 December): Boston; Symphony Hall; Guy
Maier and Lee Pattison, pianos; Boston Symphony
Orchestra; Serge Koussevitsky, conductor
(Concerto for 2 pianos and orchestra). See :
B290,B388,B389,B435

W12c. 1929 (5 September): London; Queen's Hall; Ethel
Bartlett and Rae Robertson, pianos; Henry Wood
Symphony Orchestra; Henry J. Wood, conductor
(Revised version). See: B67

W12d. 1952 (17 September): Manchester; BBC Studios;
Ethel Bartlett and Rae Robertson, pianos; BBC
Northern Orchestra; John Hopkins, conductor
(Final version).

W12e. 1969 (16 August): London; Royal Albert Hall;
Phyllis Sellick and Cyril Smith, pianos; BBC
Symphony Orchestra; Arthur Bliss, conductor
(Concerto for Two Pianos (3 Hands) and
Orchestra).

W13. CONCERTO FOR VIOLIN AND ORCHESTRA (1953-54;
Novello; 40 min.) See: B129,B259

2+1.1.2.2/3.2.3.0/timp/perc (1)/hp/strings
Commissioned by the British Broadcasting
Corporation
Dedicated to Alfredo Campoli

Location of manuscript: Lady Bliss, London

<u>Premiere</u>

W13a. 1955 (11 May): London; Royal Festival Hall; Alfredo Campoli, violin; BBC Symphony Orchestra; Malcolm Sargent, conductor. <u>See</u>: B9,B366

W14. <u>CONCERTO FOR VIOLONCELLO AND ORCHESTRA</u> (1969-70; Novello; 26 min.) <u>See</u>: B238

2+1.1.2.2/2.2.0.0/timp/hp/cel/strings
Dedicated to Mstislav Rostropovich
Location of manuscript: Lady Bliss, London

<u>Premieres</u>

W14a. 1970 (24 June): Snape; The Maltings; Mstislav Rostropovich, 'cello; English Chamber Orchestra; Benjamin Britten, conductor. <u>See</u>:B277,B417

W14b. 1972 (29 September): London; Queen Elizabeth Hall; Julian Lloyd Webber, 'cello; Chanticleer Orchestra; Ruth Gipps, conductor

<u>Other selected performances</u>

W14c. 1984 (11 March): Santa Barbara California; The Arlington; Ofra Harnoy; 'cello; Santa Barbara Symphony Orchestra; Frank Collura, conductor.

W15. <u>DISCOURSE FOR ORCHESTRA</u> (1957; Novello; 20 min.)

3.2+1.2.2+1/4.3.3.0/timp/perc(2) /hp/strings
Commissioned by the Louisville Orchestra
Dedicated to the Louisville Orchestra
Location of manuscript: Lady Bliss, London

<u>Premiere</u>

W15a. 1957 (23 October): Louisville; Columbia Auditorium; Louisville Orchestra; Robert Whitney, conductor.

<u>Other selected performances</u>

W15b. 1965 (28 September): London, Royal Festival Hall; London Symphony Orchestra; Arthur Bliss, conductor (Revised version). <u>See</u>: B54

W16. <u>EDINBURGH:OVERTURE FOR ORCHESTRA</u> (1956; Novello; 10 min.)

2+1.2.2.2/4.2.3.0/timp/perc (3)/hp/strings
Commissioned by the 10th Edinburgh Festival
Location of manuscript: Lady Bliss, London

<u>Premiere</u>

W16a. 1956 (20 August): Edinburgh; Usher Hall; Royal
        Philharmonic Orchestra; Arthur Bliss, conductor.
        See: B15

W17. ELIZABETHIAN SUITE FOR STRING ORCHESTRA (1923;
     unpublished)

        Location of manuscript: unable to trace

W18. FIRE DANCE (SINDING - arranged BLISS) (1921;
     unpublished)

        Unable to trace instrumentation
        Location of manuscript: Unable to trace

Premiere

W18a. 1921 (4 July): London; Coliseum; unable to trace
        orchestra and conductor involved.  See:B337,B419

W19. HYMN TO APOLLO (1926; Universal Edition; 14 min.)

        2+1.1+1.2.2/4.2.3.0/timp/perc (2)/hp/cel/strings
        Dedicated (in original version only) to Fritz
        Reiner and the Cincinnati Orchestra
        Location of manuscripts: University Library,
        Cambridge (original); University Library,
        Cambridge (revised)

Premieres

W19a. 1926 (28 November): Amsterdam; Concertgebouw;
        Concertgebouw Orchestra; Pierre Monteux,
        conductor. See: B99

W19b. 1927 (27 January): London; Queen's Hall; Royal
        Philharmonic Orchestra; Pierre Monteux,
        conductor. See: B77

W20. INTRODUCTION AND ALLEGRO (1926; Curwen/Boosey &
     Hawkes; 12 mins.)

        2+1.2+1.2+1.2+1/4.3.3.1/timp/perc (1)/hp/strings
        Dedicated to Leopold Stokowski and the
        Philadelphia Orchestra
        Location of manuscript: The FitzWilliam Museum,
        Cambridge (original)

Premiere

W20a. 1926 (8 September): London; Queen's Hall; New
        Queen's Hall Orchestra; Arthur Bliss, conductor.
        See: B69,B211

Other selected performances

W20b. 1928 (19 October): Philadelphia; Academy of Music;
        Philadelphia Orchestra; Leopold Stokowski,
        conductor.

W21. <u>MARCH OF HOMAGE IN HONOUR OF A GREAT MAN</u> (1961-62; unpublished; 4½ min.)

> 2+2.2.2.2/4.2.3.1/timp/perc (4)/strings
> Location of manuscript: Lady Bliss, London

<u>Premiere</u>

W21a. 1962 (30 March): London; BBC Maida Vale Studio 1; BBC Symphony Orchestra; Arthur Bliss, conductor. A recording of this performance was subsequently broadcast on the morning of 30 January 1965, prior to the broadcasting of Sir Winston Churchill's state funeral. <u>See</u> : B11

W22. <u>MEDITATIONS ON A THEME BY JOHN BLOW</u> (1955; Novello; 30 min.) <u>See</u>: B:16,B266,B441

> 3+3.2+1.2+1.2+1/4.3.3.0/timp/perc (4)/hp/strings
> Commissioned by the City of Birmingham Symphony Orchestra, with funds provided by the Feeney Trust
> Dedicated to the City of Birmingham Symphony Orchestra and its conductor, Rudolf Schwarz
> Location of manuscript: Music Library, University of Birmingham

<u>Premieres</u>

W22a. 1955 (13 December): Birmingham; the Town Hall; City of Birmingham Symphony Orchestra; Rudolf Schwarz, conductor. <u>See</u>: B59,B324

W22b. 1956 (13 February): London; Royal Festival Hall; City of Birmingham Symphony Orchestra; Rudolf Schwarz, conductor

W23. <u>MELEE FANTASQUE</u> (1921; Curwen; 12 min.)

> 2+1.2+1.2+1.2+1/4.3.3.1/timp/perc (3)/strings
> Dedicated to the memory of Claude Lovat Fraser, a great and lovable artist
> Location of manuscript: Lady Bliss, London (short score)

<u>Premiere</u>

W23a. 1921 (13 October): London; Queen's Hall; New Queen's Hall Orchestra; Arthur Bliss, conductor. <u>See</u>: B68, B429

<u>Other selected performances</u>

W23b. 1927 (27 February) Philadelphia; Academy of Music; Philadelphia Orchestra; Leopold Stokowski, conductor.

W24. <u>METAMORPHIC VARIATIONS</u> (1972; Novello; 40 min.)

3+2.2+1.2+1.2+2/4.3.2+1.1/timp/perc    (4)/cel/hp
/strings
Commissioned by the Croydon Arts Festival
Dedicated to George and Ann Dannatt in token of
a long and cherished friendship
Location of manuscripts: George and Ann Dannatt

Premiere

W24a. 1973 (21 April): Croydon; Fairfield Hall; London
Symphony Orchestra; Vernon Handley, conductor.
See: B224, B236

W25. MUSIC FOR STRINGS (1935; Novello; 23 min.) See:
B306

Scored for strings
Dedicated to Rachel and Ernest Makower
Location of manuscript: Lady Bliss, London

Premieres

W25a. 1935 (11 August): Salzburg; Grossen Saal des
Mozarteums, Vienna Philharmonic Orchestra;
Adrian Boult, conductor.

W25b. 1935 (5 November): London; Lancaster House; London
Philharmonic Orchestra; Malcolm Sargent,
conductor.

Other selected performances

W25c. 1961 (15 September): London, Royal Opera House,
Covent Garden; Covent Garden Orchestra; John
Lanchbery conductor (Diversions - ballet).

W26. THE PHOENIX - MARCH : HOMAGE TO FRANCE, AUGUST 1944
(1945; Novello; 6 min.)

2+2.2+1.2+1.2+1/4.3.3.1/timp/perc (2/3)/strings
Dedication: Je dedie cettre oevre musicale a la
France avec l'expression des mes hommages les
plus repecteux. J'ai choisi le titre de The
Phoenix, e'tant donne que, pour moi, il
symbolise la vie imperissable et la beaute
transcendante de la France.
Location of manuscript: Lady Bliss, London

Premieres

W26a. 1945 (11 March): Paris; unable to trace venue;
Premiere Orchestra de Concerts du Conservatoire;
Charles Munch, conductor.

W26b. 1945 (23 May): London; London Philharmonic
Orchestra; Charles Munch, conductor. See:B28

Other selected performances

W26c. 1981 (8 March): Lewisham; Concert Hall; Lewisham
Concert Band; Joseph Proctor, conductor ( Military Band arrangement).

W27. PROCESSIONAL (1953; Novello; 8 min.)

3.2.2.2+1/4.3.3.1/timp/perc (1)/organ/strings
Commissioned for performance in Westminster
Abbey, on the occasion of the Coronation of
Queen Elizabeth II, 2 June 1953 to accompany the
procession of H.M. Queen Elizabeth, the Queen
Mother from the West Door of the Abbey
Location of manuscript: unable to trace

Premiere

W27a. 1953 (2 June): London; Westminster Abbey;
Coronation Orchestra; Osborne Peasgood, organ;
Adrian Boult, conductor.

Other selected performances

W27b. 1954 (24 February): London; Westminster Abbey;
London Philharmonic Orchestra; William McKie,
organ; Arthur Bliss, conductor.

W28. SET OF ACT TUNES AND DANCES (PURCELL-ARRANGED
BLISS) (1919; Curwen/Faber; 8 min.)

Scored for strings
Location of manuscript: unable to trace

Premiere

W28a. 1919 (5 October): Hammersmith; Lyric Theatre;
Hammersmith Musical Society Orchestra; Arthur
Bliss, conductor.

W29. SIGNATURE AND INTERLUDE TUNE FOR ABC TELEVISION
(1956; unpublished; 2 min.)

2.2.2.2/4.2.3.0/timp/perc (1)/strings
Commissioned by ABC Television
Location of manuscript: Lady Bliss, London

Premiere

Unable to trace

W30. TWO STUDIES FOR ORCHESTRA (1920; unpublished; 14½
min.)

1+1.1+1.2+1.2+1/4.2.3.1/timp/perc
(2)/hp/cel/strings
Location of manuscript: Lady Bliss, London

Premiere

W30a. 1921 (17 February): London; Royal College of
      Music; New Queen's Hall Orchestra; Arthur Bliss,
      conductor. See: B263, B430

W31. TWONE, THE HOUSE OF FELICITY (1923; unpublished)

        Unable to trace instrumentation
        Location of manuscript: unable to trace

    Premiere

W31a. 1923 (15 March): London; Aeolian Hall; Gossens
      Small Orchestra; Eugene Gossens, conductor.
      See:B97

W32. YOUR QUESTIONS ANSWERED (1944; unpublished; 44
sec.)

        0.2.2.2/4.2.3.0/timp/perc (1)/strings
        Commissioned by the BBC
        Location of manuscript: Lady Bliss, London

    Premiere

W32a. 1944 (2 March): London; Broadcasting House; BBC
      Symphony Orchestra; Clarence Raybould, conductor
      - having been previously recorded on 25 February
      1944.

IV.  CHAMBER AND SOLO INSTRUMENTAL MUSIC

W33. ALLEGRO : For two Violins, Viola and Piano
(1923-24; unpublished)

        Location of manuscript: Lady Bliss, London

    Premiere

        Unable to trace

W34. ANDANTE TRANQUILLO E LEGATO: For unaccompanied
Clarinet (1926-27; unpublished)

        Location of manuscript: unable to trace

    Premiere

W34a. 1927 (19 January): London; Court House (Marylebone
      Lane); Frederick Thurston, clarinet. See: B22

W35. BLISS - One Step: For solo Piano (1923; Novello; 2
min.)

        Dedicated to Corelli Windeatt and his orchestra
        Location of manuscript: unable to trace

    Premiere

        Unable to trace

W36. <u>CHORAL PRELUDE: DAS ALTE JAHRE VERGANGEN 1ST</u> (J.S. BACH - arranged BLISS for solo Piano) (1932; Oxford University Press; 1½ min.)

> Dedicated to Harriet Cohen
> Location of manuscripts: Music Department, the Jewish National and University Library, Jerusalem

<u>Premiere</u>

W36a. 1932 (17 October): London; Queen's Hall; Harriet Cohen, piano.

W37. <u>CONVERSATIONS</u> : For Flute (and Bass Flute), Oboe (and Cor Anglais) Violin, Viola and Cello (1920; Goodwin and Tabb; 14 min.)

> Dedicated to the New Instrumental Quintet
> Location of manuscript: Lady Bliss, London

<u>Premiere</u> (first public performance)

W37a. 1921 (20 April): London; Aeolian Hall; The New Instrumental Quintet with Charles Souper and J.A. Macdonagh. <u>See</u>: B4,B32,B50,B98,R219

W38. <u>ELEGIAC SONNET</u>: For Tenor, Two Violins, Viola, Cello, and Piano (1954; Novello; 8 min.)

> Text by C.Day-Lewis (1904-1972)
> Dedicated to the memory of Noel Mewton-Wood
> Location of manuscript: unable to trace

<u>Premiere</u>

W38a. 1955 (28 January): London; Wigmore Hall; Peter Pears, tenor; Zorian String Quartet; Benjamin Britten, piano. <u>See</u>: B367

W39. <u>FUGUE</u>: for String Quartet (1916; unpublished) <u>See</u>: B64

> Location of manuscript: unable to trace

<u>Premiere</u>

> Unable to trace

W40. <u>INTERMEZZO</u>: For Solo Piano (c.1912; Stainer and Bell; 4 min.)

> Location of manuscript: unable to trace

<u>Premiere</u>

> Unable to trace

W41. <u>KAREN'S PIECE</u>: For Solo Violin and Piano (1939-40; unpublished)

Location of manuscript: Lady Bliss, London

<u>Premiere</u>

Unable to trace

W42. <u>MARCH AND VALSE DES FLEURS</u> (TCHAIKOVSKY - arranged BLISS for Clarinet and Cello) (c.1907; unpublished)

Location of manuscript: unable to trace

<u>Premiere</u>

W42a. 1908 (17 January): London; 21 Holland Park, Bayswater; Kennard Bliss, clarinet; Howard Bliss, piano.

W43. <u>MASKS</u>: Four Pieces for Solo Piano (1924; Curwen; 10 min.)

Dedicated to Felix Goodwin
Location of manuscript: unable to trace

<u>Premiere</u>

W43a. 1926 (2 February): London; Faculty of Arts Gallery; Arthur Benjamin, piano. <u>See</u>: B73

W44. <u>MAY-ZEEH</u>: Valse for Solo Piano (c. 1910; Gould; 2½ min.)

Dedicated a son amie MW
Location of manuscript: unable to trace

<u>Premiere</u>

Unable to trace

W45. <u>MINIATURE SCHERZO</u>: For Solo Piano, and founded on a phrase from Mendelssohn's Violin Concerto (1969; Novello; 1 min.)

Commissioned by the Musical Times for its 125th year
Dedicated to Marguerite Wolff
Location of manuscript: Lady Bliss, London

<u>Premiere</u>

W45a. 1969 (1 June): London; Broadcasting House (BBC); Marguerite Wolff, piano.

W46. <u>MUSIC FOR A PRINCE</u> : Contribution to the composite work - Theme from the Processional Interlude (played at Caernafon Castle, 1 July 1969: W167) arranged for Cello and Piano, Trumpet and Piano, or Cello, Trumpet and Piano (1970; unpublished)

Commissioned by The Performing Right Society
Dedicated to H.R.H. The Prince of Wales

Location of manuscript: H.R.H. The Prince of Wales

Premiere

W46a. 1985 (29 April): Rome; Villa Wolkonsky; Antonio Lysy, cello; David Short, trumpet; Charles Axworthy, piano.

W47. PLAY A PENTA : For Violin, Chime Bars and Piano (1971; unpublished; 1 min.)

Commissioned by Mary Priestley for use in music therapy
Dedicated to Mary and her children
Location of manuscript: Mary Priestley, London

Premiere

W47a. Unable to trace any date: London; St. Bernard's Psychiatric Hospital; Mary Priestley, violin; Marjorie Wardle, piano, with patients of St. Bernard's on chime bars.

W48. PRAELUDIUM : For Organ and optional Timpani and Percussion (1971; World Library Publications; 8½ min.)

Dedicated to Fred Tulan, friend and artist
Location of manuscript: Lady Bliss, London

Premieres

W48a. 1971 (24 November): Harvard University; Romansque Hall Busch-Reisinger Museum; Fred Tulan, organ. No percussion included.

W48b. 1972 (27 July): London; Westminster Abbey; Inez Pope, organ; James Blades, David Corkhill and Teresa Corbett, percussion; Douglas Guest, conductor.

W49. QUARTET : For Piano, Clarinet, Cello and Timpani (c.1904; unpublished)

Location of manuscript: unable to trace

Premiere

W49a. Unable to trace any date: Bilton Grange Preparatory School; Arthur Bliss, piano; Kennard Bliss, clarinet; unable to trace the cellist or timpani player.

W50. QUARTET : For Violin, Viola, Cello and Piano (1915; Novello but later withdrawn)

Dedicated to my friend Madame Lily Henkel and to her Quartet
Location of manuscript: unable to trace

Premiere

W50a. 1915 (22 April): London; Steinway Hall; Arthur
      Beckwith, violin; Lionel Tertis, viola; Herbert
      Withers, cello; Mrs. H. Withers, piano. See :
      B330,B396

W51. QUARTET NO 1 in A MAJOR : For 2 Violins, Viola and
     Cello (c.1914; Stainer and Bell; 28 min.)

     Dedicated to Edward J. Dent
     Location of manuscript: unable to trace

     Premiere

W51a. 1914 (30 May): Cambridge; University Music Club;
      T.H. Marshall, violin; S.W. Terrell, violin; H.
      Gardner, viola; J.H. Bliss, cello.

     Other selected performances

W51b. 1914 (9 June): Cambridge; Gonville and Caius
      College; T.H. Marshall, violin; S.W. Terrell,
      violin; H. Gardner, viola, J.H. Bliss, cello.

W51c. 1914 (7 July): London; 21 Holland Park, Bayswater;
      Nettie Carpenter, violin; Eugene Goossens Jnr.,
      violin; E. Yonge, viola; J.H. Bliss, cello.

W51d. 1915 (25 June): London; Aeolian Hall; A. Beckwith,
      violin; E. Goossens Jnr., violin; R. Jeremy,
      viola; C. Sharpe, cello. See: B3,B18,B41,B414

W52. QUARTET [No 2] : For 2 Violins, Viola and Cello
     (1923-4; unpublished; 16 min.)

     Location of manuscript: Lady Bliss, London

     Premiere

     Unable to trace

W53. QUARTET [No 3] : For 2 Violins, Viola and Cello
     (1940-41; Novello - published at No.1.; 30 min.)
     See : B346

     Dedicated to Mrs. Elizabeth Sprague Coolidge
     Location of manuscript: Library of Congress,
     Washington D.C. (original and revised versions)

     Premieres

W53a. 1941 (13 January): New York; Public Library; The
      Coolidge Quartet. First three movements only.

W53b. 1941 (9 April): Berkeley (University of
      California): Wheeler Hall Auditorium; The Pro
      Arte String Quartet (Revised Version).

W53c. 1941 (27 March): London; The National Gallery; The
     Griller String Quartet.

W54. QUARTET [No.4] : For 2 Violins, Viola and Cello
     (1950; Novello - published as No.2.; 30 min.)

     Dedicated to the Griller String Quartet
     Location of manuscript: Berkeley Music Library,
     University of California

     Premieres

W54a. 1950 (1 September): Edinburgh; Freemasons Hall;
     The Griller String Quartet. See: B26

     Other selected performances

W54b. 1972 (16 July): Cheltenham; Town Hall; Academy of
     St. Martin-in-the-Fields; Neville Marriner,
     conductor. (Two Contrasts for String Orchestra).
     See : B226

W55. QUINTET FOR CLARINET, TWO VIOLINS, VIOLA AND CELLO
     (1931-2; Novello; 26 min.) See: B207,255

     Dedicated to Bernard van Dieren
     Location of manuscript: Lady Bliss, London

     Premieres

W55a. 1932 (19 December): London; Hampstead (the
     composer's home); The Kutcher Quartet; Frederick
     Thurston, clarinet. See: B309

W55b. 1933 (17 February): London; Wigmore Hall; The
     Kutcher Quartet; Frederick Thurston, clarinet.
     See: B38

W56. QUINTET FOR OBOE, TWO VIOLINS, VIOLA AND CELLO
     (1927; Oxford University Press; 20 min.)

     Dedicated to Mrs Elizabeth Sprague Coolidge
     Location of manuscript: Library of Congress,
     Washington D.C.

W56a. 1927 (11 September): Venice; the Great Hall of the
     Conservatorio Benedetto Marcello; Leon Goossens,
     oboe; The Venetian Quartet. See: B21

W56b. 1928 (15 October): London; Arts Theatre Club; Leon
     Goossens, oboe; The Vienna Quartet.

Other selected performances

W56c. 1969 (30 October): Perth (Australia), Perth
     Theatre; Scottish Ballet (Frontier - ballet).

W56d. 1969 (26 November): London; Sadler's Wells
     Theatre; Scottish Ballet (Frontier - ballet).

W57. <u>QUINTET FOR TWO VIOLINS, VIOLA, CELLO AND PIANO</u>
(1919; unpublished)

> Dedicated to the City of Bath and three friends
> met therein: Sir Hugh Miller, Lady Stuart of
> Wortley and Leo. F. Schuster
> Location of manuscript: unable to trace

Premieres

W57a. 1919 (26 November): Paris; La Salle Gaveau; the
Philharmonic String Quartet; Arthur Bliss,
piano.

W57b. 1920 (27 April): London; Aeolin Hall; the
Philharmonic String Quartet; Arthur Bliss,
piano. <u>See</u> : B53

W58. <u>THE ROUT TROT</u>: For Solo Piano (1927; Novello; 1½
min.)

> Location of manuscript: Unable to trace

Premiere

W58a. 1927 (31 May): London; H.M. Theatre; Lew Leslie's
review <u>White Birds</u> with music and lyrics by
George W. Meyer; Orchestra arranged by Will
Vodery; Julian Jones, music director

W59. <u>SONATA FOR PIANO</u> (1952; Novello; 21-22 min.)

> Dedicated to Noel Mewton-Wood
> Location of manuscript: unable to trace

Premiere

W59a. 1953 (24 April): London; Broadcasting House; Noel
Mewton-Wood, piano. <u>See</u> : B271

W60. <u>SONATA FOR VIOLA AND PIANO</u> (1933; Oxford University
Press; 27 min.) <u>See</u> : B257

> Commissioned by Lionel Tertis
> Dedicated to Lionel Tertis - in admiration
> Location of manuscript: unable to trace

Premieres

W60a. 1933 (9 May): London; Hampstead (the composer's
home); Lionel Tertis, viola; Solomon, piano.
<u>See</u>: B436

W60b. 1933 (3 November): London; Broadcasting House;
Lionel Tertis, viola; Solomon, piano. <u>See</u> : B60

W61. <u>SONATA FOR VIOLIN AND PIANO</u> (c.1914; unpublished)

> Location of manuscript: Lady Bliss, London

Premiere

Unable to trace

W62. STUDY : For Solo Piano (1927; Curwen; 2 min.)

Dedicated to Edwin Evans
Location of manuscript: unable to trace

Premiere

Unable to trace

W63. SUITE : For Solo Piano (c.1912; unpublished; 11½ min.)

Dedicated to my father.
Location of manuscript: Unable to trace

Premiere

Unable to trace

W64. SUITE : For Solo Piano (1925; Curwen; 17 min.)

Location of manuscript: Unable to trace. University Library, Cambridge hold the manuscript of No.2 - Polonaise, arranged and orchestrated by Bliss.

Premiere

W64a. 1926 (15 March): London, Faculty of Arts Gallery; Kathleen Long, piano.

W65. TOAST TO THE ROYAL HOUSEHOLD: For Violin, Cello and Piano (1961; unpublished; 25 secs.)

Location of manuscript: Lady Bliss, London

Premiere

W65a. 1962 (July): Edinburgh; Palace of Holyroodhouse; unable to trace violinist and cellist; Robert C. Howells, piano.

W66. TOCCATA : For Solo Piano (c.1925; Curwen; 4½ min.)

Dedicated to my wife
Location of manuscript: unable to trace

Premiere

Unable to trace

W67. TRIO FOR PIANO, CLARINET AND CELLO (C.1907; unpublished)

Location of manuscript: unable to trace

Premiere

W67a. 1908 (19 January): London; 21 Holland Park, Bayswater; Arthur Bliss, piano; Kennard Bliss, clarinet; Howard Bliss, cello.

W68. TRIPTYCH : For Solo Piano (1970; Novello; 14 min.)

   Dedicated in gratitude and admiration to Louis Kentner
   Location of manuscript: Lady Bliss, London

Premiere

W68a. 1971 (21 March): London; Queen Elizabeth Hall; Louis Kentner, piano. See: B225, B235

W69. TWO INTERLUDES : For Solo Piano (1925; J.& W. Chester; 8½ min)

   Dedicated 1 - To Elizabeth Sprague Coolidge
            2 - To Ethel Roe Eichheim
   Location of manuscript: Library of Congress, Washington D.C.

Premiere

   Unable to trace

W70. TWO PIECES FOR CLARINET [IN A] AND PIANO (1913-16; Novello; 4 min.)

   Location of manuscripts: 1 - unable to trace
                            2 - Lady Bliss, London

Premiere

W70a. No.1. only : 1914 (7 February): Cambridge; University Music Club; Kennard Bliss, clarinet; M.O. Marshall, piano.

W70b. Complete: 1917 (15 February): London, Aeolian Hall; Charles Draper, clarinet; Lily Henkel, piano.

W71. VALSES FANTASTIQUES : For Solo Piano (1913; Stainer and Bell, 9 min.)

   Dedicated to A.R.R. on the front cover
             to C.R. (No. 2)
             to G.R. (No. 3)
   Location of manuscript: unable to trace

Premiere

   Unable to trace

W72. VALSE MELANCOLIQUE .... For Solo Piano (c. 1910; unpublished)

Location of manuscript: unable to trace

<u>Premiere</u>

W72a. 1911 (13 January ): London; 21 Holland Park, Bayswater; Arthur Bliss, piano.

W73. <u>A WEDDING SUITE</u> : For Solo Piano (1973; unpublished; 10 min.)

Location of manuscript: Marguerite Wolff, London

<u>Premiere</u>

W73a. 1974 (11 January): London; Decca Studios; Marguerite Wolff, piano.
This recording was subsequently played at the wedding reception of Sir Arthur Bliss's half-sister, Enid Frame-Thomson, at 8 The Lane, St. John's Wood on 18 January 1974.

V.   <u>VOCAL MUSIC</u>

W74. <u>AUBADE FOR CORONATION MORNING</u> : For two Soprano Soli and unaccompanied Mixed Chorus (1953; Stainer & Bell/Novello; 6½ min.) Written as a contribution to <u>A Garland for the Queen</u>.

Commissioned by The Arts Council of Great Britain, to mark the occasion of the Coronation of H.M. Queen Elizabeth II
Dedicated by gracious permission to Her Majesty Queen Elizabeth II
Location of manuscript: unable to trace
Text by Henry Reed

<u>Premiere</u>

W74a. 1953 (1 June): London; Royal Festival Hall; Cambridge University Madrigal Society and Golden Age Singers; Boris Ord, conductor. <u>See</u>: B208, B364

W75. <u>THE BEATITUDES</u> : Cantata for Soprano and Tenor Soli, Mixed Chorus, Organ and Orchestra (1960-1; Novello; 50 min.)

2+2.2.2.2/4.2.3.1/timp/perc(2)/hp(2)/org/strings
Commissioned by The Coventry Cathedral Festival Committee for the 1962 Festival of Re-dedication
Dedicated to my grand-daughter, Susan, born 10 May 1955
Location of manuscript: University Library, Cambridge
Text selected and arranged by Arthur Bliss and Christopher Hassall

<u>Premieres</u>

W75a. 1962 (25 May): Coventry, Coventry Theatre; Jennifer Vyvyan, soprano; Richard Lewis, tenor; Coventry Cathedral Festival Choir; BBC Symphony Orchestra; Arthur Bliss, conductor. See B13, B382

W75b. 1963 (16 February): London; Central Hall Westminster; Jennifer Vyvyan, soprano; Gerald English, tenor; Kensington Symphony Choir and Orchestra; Leslie Head, conductor

W76. BIRTHDAY SONG FOR A ROYAL CHILD : For unaccompanied Mixed Chorus (1959; Novello; 3 min.) Written to celebrate the birth of H.R.H. Prince Andrew, Duke of York, 19 February 1960.

Location of manuscript: The Royal Library
Text by Cecil Day Lewis

Premiere

W76a. 1959 (31 December): London; Memorial Hall Farringdon; BBC Chorus; Leslie Woodgate, conductor. See: B93.
A recording of this performance was subsequently broadcast on the morning of Saturday 20 February 1960 in the BBC's Light Programme.

W77. CRADLE SONG FOR A NEWBORN CHILD : For Mixed Chorus and Harp (or Piano) (1963; Novello; 3½ min.) Written to celebrate the birth of H.R.H. Prince Edward, 10 March 1964.

Location of manuscript: University Library, Cambridge
Text by Eric Crozier

Premiere

W77a. 1964 (5 March): London; BBC Maida Vale 1 Studio; BBC Chorus; Renata F. Feheffel-Stein, harp; Peter Gellhorn, conductor.
A recording of this performance was subsequently broadcast on the morning of Wednesday 11 March 1964 in the BBC's Home Service.

W78. THE ENCHANTRESS: Scena for Contralto and Orchestra (1951; Novello; 17 min.) See: B249

Solo contralto; 2+1.2+1.0.0/4.2.3.0/timp/perc(1) /hp/strings
Dedicated to Kathleen Ferrier
Location of manuscript: Lady Bliss, London
Text adapted from Theocritus by Henry Reed

Premieres

W78a. 1951 (2 October): Manchester; BBC Studio; Kathleen Ferrier, contralto; BBC Northern Orchestra; Charles Groves, conductor.

W78b. 1952 (6 April): London; Royal Festival Hall;
      Kathleen Ferrier, contralto; London Symphony
      Orchestra; Hugo Rignold, conductor.
      See: B27,B318

W79.  GOD SAVE THE QUEEN : Arranged for Mixed Chorus
      and Orchestra (1969; Novello; 3 min.)

          3+1.3+1.3+1.3+1/4.3.3.1/timp/perc (2)/strings
          Location of manuscript: Lady Bliss, London

      Premiere

W79a. 1969 (21 October): Burlington; Memorial
      Auditorium (University of Vermont); Royal
      Choral Society and Players; Wyn Morris,
      conductor. See: B40 (The opening concert of
      Royal Choral Society's American tour, October
      1969)

W80.  THE GOLDEN CANTATA ('MUSIC IS THE GOLDEN FORM') :
      Cantata for Tenor Solo, Mixed Chorus and
      Orchestra (1963; Novello; 28 min.)

          3+3.2.2.2/4.3.3.1/timp/perc(3+)/cel/hp/organ
          pedal/strings
          Commissioned by the Cambridge University
          Musical Society to mark the Quincentenary
          Celebrations of the first recorded degree in
          music being awarded by Cambridge University in
          1464
          Dedicated to the C.U.M.S. 1964
          Location of manuscript: Lady Bliss, London
          Text by Kathleen Raine

      Premiere

W80a. 1964 (18 February): Cambridge; The Guildhall;
      Wilfred Brown, tenor; Cambridge University
      Musical Society Chorus and Orchestra; Arthur
      Bliss, conductor. See: B416

W81.  LORD, WHO SHALL ABIDE IN THY TABERNACLE? : Anthem
      for Mixed Chorus and Organ with Four Trumpets in
      the last verse (1968; Novello; 4½ min.)

          Commissioned by Dr. Neville E. Wallbank and
          Sir John Russell [Honorary Registrar of the
          Imperial Society of Knights Bachelor] for the
          Dedication of the Knights Bachelor Shrine at
          the Church of St. Bartholomew-the-Great,
          Smithfield
          Location of manuscript: Lady Bliss, London
          Text from the Book of the Psalms

      Premiere

W81a. 1968 (10 July): London; Church of St.
      Bartholomew-the-Great, Smithfield; the Choir

of St. Bartholomew-the-Great; Maurice Barrett, organ; Brian Brockless, conductor.

W82.    MAR PORTUGUES: For unaccompanied Mixed Chorus (1973; Novello; 3 min.)

> Commissioned by the Rt. Hon. Edward Heath when Prime Minister - April/May 1973
> Dedicated to commemorate the 600th Anniversary of the Anglo-Portuguese Alliance
> Location of manuscript: Portugal. It was taken there after being presented to Dr. Caetano by Edward Heath on the occasion of the dinner to mark the sixth centenary of the Anglo-Portuguese Alliance
> Text by Fernando Pessoa, in free translation by Alan Goddison

Premiere

W82a.    1973 (16 July): Greenwich; Royal Naval College - the Painted Hall; St. Margaret's Singers; Martin Neary, conductor. See: B298

W83.    MARY OF MAGDALA : Cantata for Contralto and Bass soli, Mixed Chorus and Orchestra (1962; Novello; 27 min.)

> 2+1.2.1.1/2.2.0.0/timp/perc (2)/hp/strings
> Commissioned by the City of Birmingham Symphony Orchestra, with funds provided by the Feeney Trust
> Dedicated to the memory of Christopher Hassall, died 25 April 1963
> Location of manuscript: Music Library, University of Birmingham/Lady Bliss, London
> Text by Christopher Hassall

Premiere

W83a.    1963 (2 September): Worcester; Cathedral Church of Christ and St. Mary; Norma Proctor, contralto; John Carol Case, baritone; Three-Choirs Festival Chorus; City of Birmingham Symphony Orchestra; Arthur Bliss, conductor. See: B44,B215

W83b    1969 (14 June): London; Queen Elizabeth Hall; Meriel Dickinson, contralto; Neil Howlett, baritone; London Orpheus Choir; London Orpheus Orchestra; James Gaddarn, conductor.

W84.    MORNING HEROES: Symphony for Orator, Mixed Chorus and Orchestra (1929-30; Novello; 60 min.) See: B112,B217

> 3+1.3+1.3+1.3+1/4.3.3.1/timp(2)/perc(2)/hp/strings
> Commissioned by the Norfolk and Norwich 33rd Triennial Music Festival

Dedicated to the memory of my brother FRANCIS
KENNARD BLISS and all other comrades killed in
battle
Location of manuscript: University Library,
Cambridge
Text adapted from Homer, Walt-Whitman, Li Tai
Po, Wilfred Owen and Robert Nichols

### Premieres

W84a.    1930 (22 October): Norwich; St. Andrew's Hall;
Basil Maine, orator; Festival Chorus; Queen's
Hall Orchestra; Arthur Bliss, conductor. See
: B52, B61, B275

W84b.    1931 (25 March): London; Queen's Hall; Basil
Maine, orator; National Chorus; BBC Symphony
Orchestra; Arthur Bliss conductor. See: B12,
B209, B314

W85.    MORTLAKE ('CHRIST IS ALIVE'): Hymn Tune for
Unison Chorus and Organ (1969, Walton Music
Corporation; 2 min.)

Commissioned by Lee Hastings Bristol Jnr.
[General Editor of More Hymns and Spiritual
Songs, one of a two-part supplement to the
American Episcopal Hymal of 1940] on behalf of
the Joint Commission on Church Music
Location of manuscripts: unable to trace
Text by Brian Wren

### Premiere

W85a.    1974 (15 May): London; Westminster Abbey; Choir
from the Royal College of Music; John Wilson,
conductor.

W86.    O GIVE THANKS UNTO THE LORD: Anthem for Mixed
Chorus and Organ (1964-5; Novello; 5 min.)

Commissioned by the Dame of Sark for the
Thanksgiving Service to commemorate the 400th
Anniversary of the granting of the Royal
Charter to the Fief of Sark, 1565-1965
Location of manuscript: unable to trace
Text from the Book of the Psalms

### Premiere

W86a.    1965 (8 August): Sark (Channel Islands); Parish
Church of St. Peter; Resident Church Choir and
the Westminster Singers; Bernard Wiltshire,
organist/conductor.

W87.    ODE FOR SIR WILLIAM WALTON: For Soprano,
Contralto and Bass Soli (from the Choir) and
unaccompanied Mixed Chorus (1972; unpublished; 5½
min.)

Commissioned by the Rt. Hon Edward Heath, Prime Minister 1970-1974, to be performed at the dinner, held at 10 Downing Street, to mark the occasion of Sir William Walton's 70th birthday (29 March 1972)
Location of manuscript: Lady Walton
Text by Paul Dehn

Premiere

W87a.   1972 (29 March): London; 10 Downing Street; Martin Neary Singers, Martin Neary, conductor. See: B298

W88.    ONE,TWO,BUCKLE MY SHOE: A Nursery Rhyme for Girls' or Boys' Voices and Piano (1968; Novello; 1 min.)

Dedicated to the very young in the Orpington Junior Singers
Location of manuscript: Lady Bliss, London

Premiere

W88a.   1968 (30 March): Orpington (Kent); Midfield County Secondary School for Girls, St. Paul's Cray; Orpington Junior Singers, Iris Claydon, piano; Sheila Mossman, conductor.

W89.    PASTORAL: LIE STREWN THE WHITE FLOCKS: For Mezzo Soprano, Mixed Chorus, Flute, Timpani and String Orchestra (1928-29; Novello; 33 min.)

Commissioned by the Harold Brooke Choir
Dedicated to Edward Elgar
Location of manuscript: Lady Bliss, London
Text adapted from Ben Johnson, John Fletcher, Poliziano, Robert Nichols and Theocritus

Premiere

W89a.   1929 (8 May): London; Bishopgate Institute; Odette de Foras, mezzo soprano; Gilbert Barton, flute; Harold Brooke Choir and Orchestra; Harold Brooke, conductor.

W90.    PEN SELWOOD ('SWEET DAY, SO COOL'): Hymn Tune for Unaccompanied Mixed Chorus (1967; Cambridge University Press; 2 min.)

Commissioned by Elizabeth Poston, for the Cambridge Hymnal
Location of manuscript: unable to trace
Text by George Herbert

Premiere

Unable to trace

W91.    PRAYER OF ST.FRANCIS OF ASSISI: For unaccompanied
        Women's Chorus (1971; Novello; 4½ min.)

        Dedicated to Sheila Mossman-In Memoriam
        Location of manuscript: Lady Bliss, London

        Premieres

W91a.   1972 (11 June): Bromley; Parish church of St.
        Peter and St. Paul; Orpington Junior Singers;
        Jane Attfield, conductor.

W91b.   1972 (11 September): London; St. John's Smith
        Square; Orpington Junior Singers; Jane
        Attfield, conductor.

W92.    A PRAYER TO THE INFANT JESUS: For Soprano and
        Contralto soli and unaccompanied Women's or
        Girl's Chorus (1961; Novello; 5½ min.)

        Dedicated to Sheila Mossman and the Orpington
        Junior Singers
        Location of manuscript: Lady Bliss, London
        Text from the Prayer of Cyril of the Blessed
        Virgin to the miraculous Infant Jesus of
        Prague (in the Church of Our Lady of Vilbory,
        Prague)

        Premiere

W92a.   1968 (14 May): Orpington; Parish Church of All
        Saints; Orpington Junior Singers; Sheila
        Mossman, conductor.

W92b.   1968 (1 December): London; Westminster Theatre
        Arts Centre; Orpington Junior Singers, Sheila
        Mossman, conductor.

W93.    PUT THOU THY TRUST IN THE LORD: Introit for
        unaccompanied Mixed Double Chorus (1972; Novello;
        3 min.)

        Composed for the Silver Wedding Service of
        H.M. The Queen and H.R.H. The Duke of
        Edinburgh
        Location of manuscript: Lady Bliss, London
        Text from the Book of the Psalms

        Premiere

W93a.   1972 (20 November): London, Westminster Abbey;
        Choir of Westminster Abbey; Douglas Guest,
        conductor. See: B24

W94.    RIVER MUSIC 1967 : For unaccompanied Mixed Chorus
        (1966; Novello; 7 min.)

        Commissioned by The Greater London Council for
        the opening of the Queen Elizabeth Hall
        Location of manuscript: Lady Bliss, London

Text by Cecil Day-Lewis

Premiere

W94a.    1967 (1 March): London; Queen Elizabeth Hall;
         Ambrosian Singers; Arthur Bliss, conductor.
         See: B358, B383

W95.     SANTA BARBARA : ('HE IS THE WAY'): Hymn Tune for
         Unison Chorus and Organ (1967; Cambridge
         University Press 2½ min.)

         Commissioned by Elizabeth Poston, for the
         Cambridge Hymnal
         Location of manuscript: unable to trace
         Text by W.H. Auden

Premiere

Unable to trace

W96.     SEEK THE LORD :Anthem for Mixed Chorus and Organ
         (1955-56; Novello; 3½ min.)

         Composed for the Centenary Service of the
         Mission to Seamen
         Location of manuscript: unable to trace
         Text from the Book of Amos

Premiere

W96a.    1956 (20 February): London; Westminster Abbey;
         Choir of Westminster Abbey; Osborne Peasgood,
         organ; William McKie, conductor.

W97.     SERENADE: For Baritone Solo and Orchestra (1929;
         Oxford University Press; 25 min.)

         2+1.1.2.2/2.2.1.0/timp/perc (1)/hp/strings
         Dedicated to the composer's wife
         Location of manuscript: University Library,
         Cambridge
         Text by Edmund Spenser and Sir John Wooton

Premiere

W97a.    1930 (18 March): London; Queen's Hall; Roy
         Henderson, baritone; London Symphony
         Orchestra; Malcolm Sargent, conductor.

W98.     SHIELD OF FAITH: Cantata for Soprano and Baritone
         Soli, Mixed Chorus and Organ (1974; Novello; 35
         min.)

         Commissioned by the Dean of Windsor for the
         Quincentenary of St. George's Chapel, Windsor,
         1975
         Dedicated by Gracious Permission to Her
         Majesty Queen Elizabeth II

Location of manuscript: University Library, Cambridge
Text selected and arranged by Stephen Verney from William Dunbar, George Herbert, Alexander Pope, Alfred, Lord Tennyson and T. S. Eliot

### Premieres

W98a.  1975 (26 April): Windsor; St. George's Chapel; Jennifer Smith, soprano; John Carol Case, baritone; Bach Choir; Richard Popplewell, organ; David Willcocks, conductor.

W98b.  1976 (30 July): London; St. Augustine's Church, Killburn; Julia Kennard, soprano; Jonathan Robarts, baritone; BBC Singers; Timothy Farrell, organ; John Poole, conductor.

W99.   SING, MORTALS! : A Sonnet for the Festival of St. Cecilia, for Mixed Chorus and Organ (1974; Novello; 5½ min.)

Commissioned by The St. Cecilia Festival Church Service Committee, 1974 for the Festival Service, held in the Church of the Holy Sepulchre, Holborn
Location of manuscript: Lady Bliss,London
Text by Richard Tydeman

### Premiere

W99a.  1974 (26 November): London; Church of the Holy Sepulchre, Holborn Viaduct; Children of the Chapel Royal, St. James' Palace and Choristers and Gentlemen of St. Paul's Cathedral and Westminster Abbey; Barry Rose, organ; Christopher Dearnley, conductor.

W100.  A SONG OF WELCOME :For Soprano and Baritone Soli, Mixed Chorus and Orchestra (1954; Novello; 16 min.)

2+2.2.2.2/4.2.3.0/timp.perc (2)/hp/strings
Composed to celebrate the return of H.M. Queen Elizabeth II and H.R.H. Prince Philip from their Royal Tour, 1954
Location of manuscript: Lady Bliss, London
Text by Cecil Day-Lewis

### Premiere

W100a.  1954 (15 May): London; Camden Studios; Joan Sutherland, soprano; Ian Wallace, baritone; BBC Chorus; BBC Concert Orchestra; Malcolm Sargent, conductor.

### Other selected performances

W100b.  1954 (29 July): London; Royal Albert Hall; Elsie Morrison, soprano; Ian Wallace, baritone; BBC

Chorus; BBC Choral Society; BBC Symphony Orchestra; Malcolm Sargent, conductor.

W101.    STAND UP AND BLESS THE LORD YOUR GOD: Anthem for Soprano and Bass Soli, Mixed Chorus and Organ (1960; Novello; 8 min.)

Composed for Llandaff Cathedral Choir on the completion of the restoration of the Cathedral after war damage
Location of manuscript: unable to trace
Text from the Books of Nehemiah, Isaiah and I Kings

Premiere

W101a.    1960 (6 August): Llandaff; Cathedral Church of St. Peter and St. Paul; Cathedral Choir; V. Anthony Lewis, organist; Robert Joyce, conductor. See: B42

W102.    THREE SONGS FOR GIRLS' OR BOYS' VOICES and Piano (1967; Novello, 6½ min.)

Dedicated to Sheila Mossman and the Orpington Junior Singers
Location of manuscript: Lady Bliss, London
Texts :    No.1 - Little Bingo: A nursery Rhyme
          No.2 - A widow bird: P.B. Shelley
                      (with piano)
          No.3 - A New Year Carol: Anon.

Premieres

W102a.    1969 (2 January): London; Queen Elizabeth Hall; Orpington Junior Singers; Sheila Mossman, conductor. No.3 only

W102b.    1969 (29 March): Orpington; Walsingham School for Girls, St. Paul's Cray; Orpington Junior Singers; Iris Clayton, piano; Sheila Mossman, conductor.

W103.    TWO BALLADS : For Childrens' or Womens' Chorus and Piano or Small Orchestra (1970; Novello; 12½ min.)

2+1.2.2.2/2.2.0.0/timp/perc (2)/hp/strings
Commissioned by the Isle of Man Arts Council for the school children of the Isle of Man
Location of manuscript: Lady Bliss, London (vocal score)
Texts    :    No.1    The    Mountain    Plover (Ushagreaisht) from The Folk Lore of the Isle of Man - A.W. Moore : No.2 Flowers in the Valley from The Atlantic Book of British and American Poetry, Vol.1 edited by Edith Sitwell

Premiere

W103a.  1971 (16 April): Douglas; Isle of Man, the Villa
        Marina;    the    Island    Schools    Choir;
        Leicestershire  Schools  Symphony  Orchestra;
        Eric Pinkett, conductor.

W104.   WHEN WILT THOU SAVE THE PEOPLE (CORN LAW RHYME):
        For Mixed Chorus and Band (1941; unpublished)

        Unable to trace instrumentation
        Commissioned by Miss Lloyd George
        Location of manuscript: unable to trace
        Text by J. Booth.

        Premiere

        Unable to trace

W105.   THE WORLD IS CHARGED WITH THE GRANDEUR OF GOD:
        Cantata  for  Mixed  Voices,  Two  Flutes,  Three
        Trumpets  and  Four  Trombones  (1969; Novello;  14
        min.)

        Commissioned by Peter Pears
        Dedicated to Peter Pears, who selected these
        poems for me
        Location of manuscript: Lady Bliss, London
        Text by Gerard Manley Hopkins

        Premieres

W105a.  1969 (27 June): Blythburgh; Parish Church of the
        Holy Trinity; Aldeburgh Festival Instrumental
        and   Choral   Ensembles;   Philip   Ledger,
        conductor.

W105b.  1973  (14  January):  London;  Wormwood  Scrubs,
        Church of St. Francis; Bach Choir; J. Miller
        Ensemble;  Douglas  Mackie  and  Wendy  Simon,
        flutes; David Willcock, conductor.

VI.  SONGS

W106.   ANGELS OF THE MIND : Song Cycle of Soprano and
        piano (1968; Novello; 17 min.)

        Commissioned  by  the  British  Broadcasting
        Corporation
        Dedicated to Kathleen Raine
        Location of manuscript: Lady Bliss, London
        Text by Kathleen Raine

        Premiere

W106a.  1969 (2 December): Lancaster; Main Hall of the
        University;  Rae  Woodland,  soprano;  Lemar
        Crawson, piano.

W107.   AT THE WINDOW: For Voice and Piano (c.1925;
        unpublished; 1 min.)

Location of manuscript: unable to trace
Text by Alfred Lord Tennyson

### Premiere

Unable to trace

W108.   AUVERGNAT : For Voice and Piano (1943; Novello; 1 min.)

Location of manuscript: unable to trace
Text by Hilaire Belloc

### Premiere

Unable to trace

W109.   THE BALLADS OF THE FOUR SEASONS : Song Cycle for Voice and Piano (1923; Composers' Music Corporation/Novello; 7½ min.)

Dedicated to Minnie Untermyer
Location of manuscript: Music Division, New York Public Library
Text by Li Po, translated by Shigeyoshi Obata

### Premiere

Unable to trace

### Other selected performances

W109a.  1960 (12 July): Cheltenham; Town Hall; Elizabeth Simon soprano; Gerald Moore, piano. Nos.1 and 4 only.

W110.   A CHILD'S PRAYER : For Voice and Piano (1926; Novello; 1 min.)

Dedicated to Barbara [the composer's elder daughter]
Location of manuscript: unable to trace
Text by Siegfried Sassoon

### Premiere

Unable to trace

W111.   THE FALLOW DEER AT THE LONELY HOUSE: For Voice and Piano (1924; Novello; 2½ min.)

Dedicated to Ursula Grenville
Location of manuscript: Lady Bliss, London
Text by Thomas Hardy

### Premiere

W111a.  1925 (5 October): London; Wigmore Hall; Elizabeth Nicol, soprano; S. Liddle, piano. See :B75

W112.  FOUR SONGS : For Voice, Violin and Piano (1927;
       Novello; 5½ min.)

           Location of manuscript: Lady Bliss, London
           (nos 1,3 and 4)
           Texts by Arthur S. Cripps, Charlotte Mew and
           L.A.G. Strong

       Premiere

W112a. 1927 (6 April): London; Grotrian Hall; Sybil
       Scanes, soprano; Paul Belinfante, violin;
       George Reeves, piano. See: B76

W113.  THE HAMMERS : For Voice and Piano (c.1915;
       unpublished; 2 min.)

           Location of manuscript: unable to trace
           Text by Ralph Hodgson

       Premiere

           Unable to trace

W114.  A KNOT OF RIDDLES: Song Cycle for Baritone and
       Eleven Instruments (1963; Novello; 17 min.)

           1+1.1.1.1/1.0.0.0/0/hp/2 vlns/vla/vc/db
           Commissioned by the British Broadcasting
           Corporation for the 1963 Cheltenham Festival
           Dedicated to William Glock [Director of Music,
           BBC]
           Location of manuscripts: Lady Bliss, London
           Text translated from the Old English of The
           Exeter Book by Kevin Crossley-Holland

       Premieres

W114a. 1963 (11 July): Cheltenham; Town Hall; John
       Shirley-Quirk, baritone; Richard Adeney,
       flute; Peter Graeme, oboe, Gervase de Peyer,
       clarinet; William Waterhouse, bassoon; Barry
       Tuckwell, horn; Osian Ellis, harp; Emanuel
       Hurwitz, violin; Ivor McMahon, violin; Cecil
       Avonowitz, viola; Terence Weil, cello; Adrian
       Beers, double bass. See: B273

W114b. 1964 (17 June): London; Victoria and Albert
       Museum; John Shirley-Quirk, baritone; members
       of the Bath Festival Orchestra; Arthur Bliss,
       conductor.

W115.  MADAME NOY: A Witchery Song for Soprano, Flute,
       Clarinet, Bassoon, Harp, Viola and Double bass
       (1918; Chester; 3½ min.)

           Dedicated to Anne Thursfield
           Location of manuscript: Fitzwilliam Museum,
           Cambridge
           Text by E.H.W. Meyerstein

Premiere

W115a.    1920 (23 June): London; Wigmore Hall; Anne
          Thursfield, soprano; instrumental ensemble;
          Arthur Bliss, conductor. See: B49

W116.     RHAPSODY : For Mezzo-soprano, Tenor, Flute,
          Clarinet, String Quartet and Double Bass (1919;
          Stainer and Bell; 7 min.) See: B35

          Dedicated to Gerald Cooper
          Location of manuscript: unable to trace
          Text: vocalise on 'ah'

Premiere

W116a.    1920 (6 October): London; Mortimer Hall; Dorothy
          Helmrich, soprano; Gerald Cooper, tenor;
          Albert Fransella, flute; Walter S. Hinchliff,
          clarinet; Wadsworth Quartet with double bass;
          Arthur Bliss, conductor. See: B301, B420

W117      RICH OR POOR : For Voice and Piano (1925-26;
          Novello; 2 min.)

          Dedicated to Lawrence Strauss
          Location of manuscript: Lady Bliss, London
          Text by W.H. Davies

Premiere

          Unable to trace

W118.     ROUT : For Soprano, Flute, Clarinet,
          Glockenspiel, Side Drum, Harp, String Quartet
          with Double bass (1920; Goodwin & Tabb; 7 min.)

          Dedicated to Grace Crawford
          Location of manuscript: unable to trace
          Text: "A medley of made-up words" by Arthur
          Bliss

Premieres

W118a.    1920 (15 December): London; 139 Piccadilly;
          Grace Crawford, soprano; Albert Fransella,
          flute; Charles Draper, clarinet; J.H. Plowman,
          percussion; Gwendolen Mason, harp; Philhar-
          monic String Quartet; Claude Hobday, double
          bass, Arthur Bliss, conductor. See: B55, B418

W118a.    1921 (4 May): London; Steinway Hall; Grace
          Crawford, soprano; instrumental ensemble
          including the Pennington String Quartet;
          Arthur Bliss, conductor.

W119.     SAILING OR FLYING? :For Voice and Piano (1970;
          unpublished; 1½ min.)

          Location of manuscript: Lady Bliss, London

Text by Winifred Williams

Premiere

Unable to trace

W120.  SEVEN AMERICAN POEMS : For Low Voice and Piano
       (1940; Boosey & Hawkes; 9½ min.) See also W128

          Dedicated to Bernhard and Irene Hoffmann, in
          whose house in Santa Barbara these songs were
          written in August 1940
          Location of manuscript: Lady Bliss, London
          (no.7 only)
          Text by Edna St. Vincent Millay (nos 1,2,3,5
          and 7) and Ellinor Wylie (nos 4 and 6)

       Premieres

W120a.  1941 (6 February): San Francisco; Museum of Art;
        Nicholas Goldschmidt, baritone; [Arthur Bliss,
        piano]

W120b.  1941 (8 November): London; Wigmore Hall; William
        Parsons, baritone; Arthur Bliss, piano.

W121.  SIMPLES:  For Voice and Piano (1932; Oxford
       University Press; 3 min.)

          Location of manuscript: unable to trace
          Text by James Joyce from Pomes Penyeach

       Premiere

W121a.  1932 (16 March): London; College of Nursing
        (Cavendish Square); un-named singer; William
        Busch, piano See: B23

W122.  THREE JOLLY GENTLEMEN: For Voice and Piano (1923;
       Composers' Music Corporation; 1 min.)

          Location of manuscript: unable to trace
          Text by Walter de la Mare

       Premiere

          Unable to trace

W123.  THREE ROMANTIC SONGS: For Voice and Piano (1921;
       Novello; 4½ min.) See: B106

          Dedicated to (No.1) Patrick Mahony
                       (No.2) Cynthia Mahony
                       (No.3) Enid Bliss
          Location of manuscript: Music Division, New
          York Public Library (No.3 only)
          Text by Walter de la Mare

       Premiere

W123a.  1922 (18 January): London; Wigmore Hall; Anne Thursfield, soprano; Arthur Bliss, piano.

W124.   THREE SONGS: For Voice and Piano (1922, revised 1972, Novello; 7 min.)

    Dedicated to Elizabeth Poston
    Location of manuscript: unable to trace
    Text by William H. Davies

Premiere

    Unable to trace

W125.   'TIS TIME I THINK BY WENLOCK TOWN: For Voice and Piano (c. 1914; unpublished; 2 min.)

    Location of manuscript: unable to trace
    Text by A.E. Housman

Premiere

    Unable to trace

W126.   THE TRAMPS: For Voice and Piano (1916; Boosey & Hawkes; 1½ min.)

    Dedicated to all Hoboes
    Location of manuscript: Lady Bliss, London
    Text by Robert Service

Premiere

    Unable to trace

W127.   TULIPS: For Voice and Piano or Guitar (1970; unpublished; 1 min.)

    Location of manuscript: Lady Bliss, London
    Text by Winifred Williams

Premiere

    Unable to trace

W128.   TWO AMERICAN POEMS: For Voice and Piano (1940; Boosey & Hawkes; 3 min.) See also W120

    Location of manuscript: Lady Bliss, London
    Text by Edna St. Vincent Millay

Premiere

    Unable to trace

W129.   TWO NURSERY RHYMES: For Soprano, Clarinet and Piano (1920; Chester: 3½ min.)

    Dedicated to (No.1) Leslie Howard
               (No.2) Charles Draper

Location of manuscript: unable to trace
Text by Frances Cornford

Premieres

W129a.  1921 (18 January): London; Gladys Moger, soprano; Frederick Thurston, clarinet; Arthur Bliss, piano [first performance only of No.1]

W129b.  1921 (26 January): London; Aeolian Hall; Gladys Moger, soprano; Frederick Thurston, clarinet; Arthur Bliss, piano. See: B48, B74

W129c.  1921 (4 May): London; Steinway Hall; Grace Crawford, soprano; Charles Draper, clarinet, Arthur Bliss, piano.

W130.  WHEN I WAS ONE AND TWENTY: Song for Voice and Piano (1924; Ricordi; 3 min.)

Location of manuscript: unable to trace
Text by A.E. Housman

Premiere

Unable to trace

W131.  THE WOMEN OF YUEH: Song Cycle for Voice and Ensemble (1923; Chester; 7½ min.)

1.1.1.1/0.0.0.0/perc (1)/2vs,va, cello,db
Dedicated to Ernest Ansermet
Location of manuscript: Lady Bliss, London
Texts by Li Po, translated by Shigeyoshi Obata

Premiere

W131a.  1923 (11 November): New York; Klaw Theatre; Lillian Gustafson soprano; Instrumental Group; Arthur Bliss, conductor.

Other selected performances

1925 (6 May): London; Grosvenor House; Mary Lohden soprano, Manlio di Veroli, piano.

VII. FILM MUSIC

W132.  THE BEGGAR'S OPERA: Musical Additions and Arrangements, realised from the original airs by John Gay, for the film. Shepperton and Denham Studios. Produced by Lord Olivier and Herbert Wilcox. Directed by Peter Brook (1952-53; unpublished). See B285

2+2.2+1.2.2/2.2.3.1/timp/perc (2)/hp/cel/string
Location of manuscript: Lady Bliss, London

Premiere

W132a.    1953 (31 May): London; Rialto Theatre, Coventry
          St; music played by the London Symphony
          Orchestra; Muir Mathieson, conductor.

### Other selected performances

W132b.    1958 (11 October): Leicester; De Montfort Hall;
          Marian Studholme, soprano; Joyce Gartside,
          mezzo-soprano; Gwent Lewis, tenor; John
          Cameron, bass; "massed choirs of Leicester";
          BBC Concert Orchestra; Arthur Bliss, conductor
          (Concert Version). See: B192, B415

W132c.    1969 (25 October): Lehigh; University; Eugene
          Gifford Grace Hall; Lehigh University Glee
          Club; Lehigh University Band; Jonathan Elkus,
          conductor (Two Songs).

W133.     CAESAR AND CLEOPATRA : Music for the film. Denham
          Studios. Produced by Gabriel Pascal (1944;
          unpublished; 35 min.)

          2+1.2+1.2.2/4.3.3.1/buccinas/timp/perc(3)/hps
          (2)/cel/male choir/strings
          Location of manuscript: University Library,
          Cambridge

### Premiere

          The film was released in December 1945 with a
          completely new score by George Auric.

W134.     CHRISTOPHER COLUMBUS: Music for the film. Denham
          Studios. Produced by A. Frank Bundy. Directed by
          David MacDonald (1949; unpublished). See: B285,
          B316

          2+2.2+1.2.3+1/4.3.3.0/timp/perc(3)/guitar
          /harpsichord/hp/mixed chorus/strings
          Location of manuscript: University Library,
          Cambridge

### Premiere

W134a.    1949 (16 June): London; Odeon Cinema, Leicester
          Square; music played by the Royal Philharmonic
          Orchestra; Muir Mathieson, conductor

### Other selected performances

W134b.    1980 (20 August): Bristol; Colston Hall; BBC
          Radio Bristol Festival Orchestra; Alistair
          Jones, conductor (Orchestral Suite).

W135.     CONQUEST OF THE AIR: Music for the film. Denham
          Studios. Produced by Alexander Korda. Directed
          by Zoltan Korda, Alexander Esway, Donald Taylor,
          Alexander Shaw, John Monk Saunders and William
          Camera Menzies (1936-37; unpublished). See: B285

Unable to trace instrumentation
Location of manuscript: unable to trace

Premiere

W135a.   1940 (20 May): London; Phoenix Theatre; music
played by the London Film Symphony Orchestra,
Muir Mathieson, conductor.

Other selected performances

W135b.   1938 (3 September): London; Queen's Hall; BBC
Symphony Orchestra; Henry J. Wood, conductor
(Orchestral Suite).

W136.    MEN OF TWO WORLDS: Music for the film.    Denham
Studios.    Produced by John Sutro.    Directed by
Thorold Dickinson (1945; unpublished). See: B285,
B316,B399

2+1.2.2+1.2+1/4.2.3.0/timp/perc(2)/cel/male
chorus/strings
Location of manuscripts: University Library,
Cambridge and Lady Bliss, London, including
Baraza, a miniature piano concerto played in
the film.

Premieres

W136a.   1946 (16 July): Dar es Salaam (Tanganyika);
Avalon Cinema; music played by the National
Symphony Orchestra; Eileen Joyce, piano; Muir
Mathieson, conductor. See: B276, B384, B451

W136b.   1946 (22 July): London; Gaumont, Haymarket.
Trade showing.

W136c.   1946 (9 September): on general release.

W137.    PRESENCE AU COMBAT: Music for the film.   Directed
by Marcel Cravenne (1945; unpublished)

2.1.2.2/2.3.3.1/timp/perc (1)/strings
Location of manuscript: University Library,
Cambridge ("France Arises" only)

Premiere

W137a.   1945 (11 December): Paris; unable to trace
cinema; music played by the National Symphony
Orchestra; Muir Mathieson, conductor.

W138.    SEVEN WAVES AWAY: Music for the film.  Denham
Studios.    Produced by John. R. Sloan.    Directed
by Richard Sale (1956; unpublished). See: B285

2+1.2.2+1.2/4.3.3.0/timp/perc
(2)/mouth-organ/strings
Location of manuscript: University Library,
Cambridge

Premiere

W138a.  1957 (8 March): London; Odeon Cinema, Leicester
        Square; music played by the Sinfonia of
        London, Muir Mathieson, conductor. See: B30

W139.   THINGS TO COME: Music for the film.  Story by
        H.G. Wells from his novel.  Denham Studios.
        Produced by Alexander Korda.  Directed by William
        Cameron Menzies (1934-35; unpublished). See:
        B285, B316

        1+1.1+1.2.2+1/2.4.2+2.1/timp/perc(2)/piano/
        hps(2)/organ/strings
        Location of manuscript: University Library,
        Cambridge ("Attack on the Moon Gun" only)

Premiere

W139a.  1936 (21 February): London; Odeon Cinema,
        Leicester Square; music played by the London
        Film Symphony Orchestra; Muir Mathieson,
        conductor.

Other selected performances

W139b.  1935 (12 September): London, Queen's Hall; BBC
        Symphony Orchestra; Arthur Bliss, conductor
        (Orchestral Suite)

W140.   WELCOME THE QUEEN: March for Orchestra. Written
        for the last section and end titles of the
        Associated British-Pathe film which celebrated
        the return of H.M. Queen Elizabeth II and H.R.H.
        Prince Philip from their Royal Tour.  Denham
        Studios.  Produced by Howard Thomas (1954;
        unpublished) See: B285

        2+1.2.2.1+1/4.3.3.1/timp/perc(3)/strings
        Location of manuscript: University Library,
        Cambridge

Premiere

W140a.  1954 (20 May): London; National Film Theatre;
        music played by the London Symphony Orchestra;
        Muir Mathieson, conductor.

Other selected performances

W140a.  1954 (19 June): London; Royal Festival Hall; BBC
        Concert Orchestra; London Light Concert
        Orchestra; Muir Mathieson, conductor
        (Arrangement for full orchestra).

VIII  INCIDENTAL MUSIC

W141.   AN AGE OF KINGS: For Orchestra. Title and End
        Music (Prelude and Postlude) to the BBC TV
        15-part series of Shakespeare's plays (Richard II

to Richard III). Produced by Peter Dews (1960; Chappell - concert band arrangement; 2 min.)

2+1.2.2.2/4.3.3.0/timp/perc (2)/piano/strings
Commissioned by the British Broadcasting Corporation
Location of manuscript: Lady Bliss, London

### Premiere

W141a. 1960 (29 March): London; BBC Maida Vale Studio-I; Royal Philharmonic Orchestra; Lionel Salter, conductor. This recording was subsequently used on Thursday 28 April 1960 when the first play (Richard II) in the series was televised.

### Other selected performances

W141b. 1966 (1 October): Lehigh; University: Eugene Gifford Grace Hall; Lehigh University Band; Jonathan Elkus, conductor (Military Band Arrangement).

W142. AS YOU LIKE IT : For Solo Voice, Chorus, Two Violins, Viola and Cello, arranged by Bliss, from late Elizabethan Sources, to Shakespeare's play. Produced by Nigel Playfair. (1919; unpublished)

Location of manuscript: unable to trace

### Premieres

W142a. 1919 (22 April): Stratford-upon-Avon; Memorial Theatre; Fanny Wadsworth and Jessie Bowater, violins; Rhoda Legge, viola; Dorothy Choules, cello; Arthur Bliss, musical director.

W142b. 1920 (21 April): Hammersmith (London); Lyric Theatre; Fanny Wadsworth and Jessie Bowater, violins; Rhoda Legge, viola; Dorothy Choules, cello; Arthur Bliss, musical director. See: B381

W143. KING SOLOMON: Incidental Music for Ira Remsen's play (1924; unpublished)

Unable to trace instrumentation
Location of manuscript: unable to trace

### Premiere

W143a. 1924 (21 March): Santa Barbara, California; Potter Theatre; unable to trace instrumentalists; Arthur Bliss, musical director. See: B392

W144. MEMORIAL CONCERT: For Orchestra. Introduction, Rehearsal Fragment, Opening of Violin Concerto and Cadenza to Trudy Bliss's radio play.

Produced for the BBC by Felix Felton (1945; K. Prowse; 8½ min.) See: B248

1.1.2.2/2.1.3.0/timp/hp/solo violin/strings
Location of manuscript: University Library, Cambridge

Premiere

W144a.   1945 (8 November): London; Broadcasting House; Henry Holst, violin; John Wills, piano, BBC Symphony Orchestra; Clarence Raybould, conductor.

Other selected performances

W144b.   1946 (11 March): London; Broadcasting House; Max Rostal, violin; John Wills, piano; BBC Symphony Orchestra; Clarence Raybould, conductor.

W144c.   1949 (31 March): London; Broadcasting House; Alfredo Campoli, violin; London Light Concert Orchestra; Michael Krein, conductor (Theme and Cadenza)

W145.    THE ROYAL PALACES OF GREAT BRITAIN: For Orchestra. Incidental Music for the BBC/ITV Film. Directed by Anthony de Lotbiniere. Naration by Kenneth Clark (1966; Chappell-concert band arrangement; 15 min.)

2+1.1.2.1/2.2.3.0/timp/perc (2)/hp/strings
Commissioned by the BBC/ITV
Location of manuscript: Lady Bliss, London

Premiere

W145a.   1966 (25 December): Film shown on BBC/ITV networks. Unable to trace when/where pre-recording took place. Music played by the Sinfonia of London; Muir Mathieson, conductor.

W146.    SUMMER DAY'S DREAM : For Oboe and Violin. Incidental Music to J.B. Priestley's play (1949; unpublished; 1½ min.)

Location of manuscript: Lady Bliss, London

Premieres

W146a.   1949 (8 August): Bradford; Prince's Theatre; unable to trace instrumentalists. See: B390

W146b.   1949 (8 September): London; St. Martin's Theatre; unable to trace instrumentalists. See: B81,B327

W147.    THE TEMPEST: Overture, Act 1, Scene 1, and Music for Act 1, Scene 2; Act 3, Scene 3; Act 4, Scene

1 to Shakespeare's play. Produced by Louis Calvert and Viola Tree (1920-21; unpublished)

0.0.0.0/0.1.1.0/timp   (5)/perc   (3/4)/grand piano/ 2 voices
Location of manuscript: Lady Bliss, London

### Premieres

W147a.  1921 (1 February): London; Aldwych Theatre; Steuart Wilson, tenor; Ivan Firth, bass; H. Jacob, piano; H. Barr, trumpet; J. Stamp, trombone; Messrs. C. Turner, A. Beckwith, F.H. Wheelhouse, J.H. Plowman and F. Deverell, timpani, marimba, gongs and drums. See: B247, B372

W147b.  1921 (8 April): London; Queen's Hall; Steuart Wilson, tenor; Topliss Green, bass; Harriet Cohen, piano; Herbert Barr, trumpet; Jesse Stamp, trombone; Messrs. C. Turner, C. Bender, J.H. Plowman, F.H. Wheelhouse and F. Deverill, timpani and percussion; Edward Clark, conductor. (Concert performance of the Overture)

W148.  WAR IN THE AIR: For Orchestra. Title and End Music to the BBC TV Series of documentary films, written and produced by John Elliot. (1954; unpublished; 1½ min.)

2.2.2.2/4.2.3.0/timp (4)/perc (2)/strings
Commissioned by the British Broadcasting Corporation
Location of manuscript: University Library, Cambridge

### Premiere

W148a.  1954 (8 November): London; Television Centre; London Symphony Orchestra; Muir Mathieson, conductor.

W148b.  1956 (7 April): London; Royal Albert Hall; Halle Orchestra and Central Band of the R.A.F.; Arthur Bliss, conductor (Salute to the R.A.F.).

## IX.  MUSIC FOR BRASS AND MILITARY BAND, INCLUDING FANFARES

W149.  THE BELMONT VARIATIONS: Theme, Six Variations and Finale for Brass Band (1962; Paxton; 11 min.) See: B284,B368

Commissioned by the National Brass Band Championships of Great Britain
Location of manuscript: Lady Bliss, London

### Premiere

W149a.  1963 (19 October): London; Royal Albert Hall;
        used as the test piece in the 1963
        Championships, the winning band being the CWS
        (Manchester) Band; Alec Mortimer, conductor
        See:B57

W150.   BIRTHDAY GREETINGS TO THE CROYDON SYMPHONY
        ORCHESTRA: For Four Horns, Three Trumpets, Three
        Trombones, Tuba, Timpani and Percussion (1971;
        Robert King Music, 1½ min.)

        Composed for the orchestra's 50th Anniversary
        Location of manuscript: unable to trace

Premiere

W150a.  1971 (15 May): Croydon; Fairfield Hall; Croydon
        Symphony Orchestra; Arthur Davison, conductor.

Other selected performances

W150b.  1974 (24 January); Santa Barbara; Granada Thea-
        tre; Santa Barbara Symphony Orchestra; Ronald
        Ondrejka, conductor (Fanfare for a Coming of
        Age).

W151.   CALL TO ADVENTURE: March for Military Band (1961;
        Chappell; 3 min.)

        Composed for the 21st Anniversary of the Air
        Training Corps
        Location of manuscript: unable to trace

Premiere

W151a.  1962 (4 February): London; Church of St. Clement
        Danes; Central Band of the RAF; Wg. Cmndr.
        J.L. Wallace, conductor.

W152.   CEREMONIAL PRELUDE: Four Horns, Three Trumpets,
        Three Trombones, Timpani, Percussion and Organ
        (1965; World Library Publications; 5 min.)

        Commissioned by the Dean of Westminster for
        the service to inaugurate the 900th
        Anniversary Celebrations of Westminster Abbey.
        It accompanied the procession of H.M. the
        Queen from the West Door to the Shrine of King
        Edward the Confessor, and then to the Stalls.
        Location of manuscript: unable to trace

Premiere

W152a.  1965(28 December): London; Westminster Abbey;
        New Philharmonic Orchestra; Simon Preston,
        organ; Arthur Bliss, conductor. See: B92

W153.   ENID'S BLAST: For Trumpet (1968; unpublished; ½
        min.)

Composed for the composer's late half-sister, Enid. To be played by friends of Enid at the opening of her Arts Festival in Carpinteria. Location of manuscript: the estate of the late Mrs. Enid Frame-Thomson, Carpinteria, California

Premiere

W153a.    Unable to trace any date. Carpinteria, California; Studio of Twin Pines Ranch; Bruce Hudson, trumpet.

Other selected performances

W153b.    1969(12 February): Carpinteria; Studio of Twin Pines Ranch; Bruce Hudson, trumpet; Roger Clarke, piano (Arrangement for trumpet and piano).

W154.    FANFARE FOR THE COMMONWEALTH ARTS FESTIVAL: For Four Trumpets, Four Trombones, Timpani and Percussion (1965; Robert King Music; 1 min.)

Written for the opening of the 1965 Commonwealth Arts Festival
Location of manuscript: unable to trace

Premiere

W154a.    1965 (16 September): London; Whitehall Banqueting Hall; Trumpeters of the Royal Military School of Music, Kneller Hall; Lieut. Col. Basil H. Brown, conductor.

Other selected performances

W154b.    1967 (19 November): London, Royal Festival Hall; brass section of the London Symphony Orchestra; Arthur Bliss, conductor (Fanfare for the Lord Mayor of London).

W155.    FANFARE FOR A DIGNIFIED OCCASION: For Soprano Trumpet, Three B-flat Trumpets; Two Tenor Trombones and Bass Trombone (1938, Boosey and Hawkes; 20 secs.)

Commissioned by Boosey & Hawkes Limited
Location of manuscript: Lady Bliss, London

Premiere

Unable to trace

W156.    FANFARE FOR HEROES: For Three Trumpets, Three Trombones, Tuba, Timpani and Cymbals (1930; Novello; 2 min.)

Written in aid of the Musicians' Benevolent Fund

Location of manuscript: Lady Bliss, London /Musicians' Benevolent Fund, London

### Premiere

W156a.    1932(26 May): London; Royal Albert Hall; combined forces of the RMSM, Kneller Hall, BBC Symphony Orchestra and the Royal Philharmonic Society Orchestra; Captn. H.E. Adkins, conductor.

W157.    FANFARE FOR THE NATIONAL FUND FOR RESEARCH INTO CRIPPLING DISEASES: For Four Trumpets and Four Trombones (1973; Novello; 1 min.)

Commissioned by The National Fund for Research into Crippling Diseases (Action Research for the Crippled Child)
Location of manuscript: Kneller Hall; Twickenham.

### Premiere

W157a.    1973 (18 October): London; St. Paul's Cathedral; Trumpets of the RMSM, Kneller Hall; D.H. MacKay, conductor. See: B96

W158.    FANFARE FOR A POLITICAL ADDRESS: For Two Clarinets, Trumpet and Speaker (1921; Goodwin & Tabb; 15 secs.)

Written for the musical journal Fanfare, edited by Leigh Henry
Location of manuscript: University Library, Cambridge

### Premiere

Unable to trace

W159.    FANFARE: THE RIGHT OF THE LINE: For Four Trumpets, Three Trombones, Timpani and Percussion (1965; Novello; 2 min.)

Composed for the 250th Anniversary of the formation of the Royal Artillery Regiment
Location of manuscript: Royal Artillery Band Library, Woolwich

### Premieres

W159a.    1966 (29 January): Hong Kong; City Hall; Herald Trumpeters of the Royal Artillery; Lt. Col. S.V. Hays, conductor.

W159b.    1966 (8 July): London; St. Paul's Cathedral; Herald Trumpeters of the Royal Artillery, Cpt. R. Quinn, conductor.

W160.    FANFARE FOR THREE TRUMPETS, THREE TROMBONES AND
         TIMPANI IN HONOUR OF SIR HENRY WOOD'S 75TH
         BIRTHDAY (1944; unpublished; 1 min.)

         Commissioned by The Musicians' Benevolent Fund
         Location of manuscript: Novello & Co. Ltd.

         Premieres

W160a.   1944 (24 March): London; Savoy Hotel; Trumpeters
         of the RMSM; Lt. Col. M. Roberts, conductor.
         See: B56

W160b.   1944 (25 March): London; Royal Albert Hall; BBC
         Symphony Orchestra and the London Symphony
         Orchestra; Sir Adrian Boult, conductor.

         Other selected performances

W160c.   1944 (10 June): London; Royal Albert Hall;
         London Philharmonic Orchestra; Basil Cameron,
         conductor. (A Birthday Fanfare).

W161.    THE FIRST GUARDS: March for Military Band (1956;
         Chappell; 6 min.)

         Composed in honour of the Tercentenary of the
         Grenadier Guards
         Location of manuscript: unable to trace

         Premiere

W161a.   1956 (2 June): London; Royal Festival Hall; Band
         of the Grenedier Guards; Arthur Bliss,
         conductor.

W162.    GALA FANFARE: (1962; Chappell; 1 min.) See B411

         Commissioned by Professor Frank Callaway for
         the opening of the VIIth British Empire and
         Commonwealth Games in Perth, Western Australia
         Location of manuscript: Lady Bliss, London
         (short score)

         Premiere

W162a.   1962 (22 November): Perth (Western Australia);
         Games Stadium, Central Band of the RAAF; Sq.
         Ldr. L.H. Hicks, conductor.

W163.    GREETINGS TO A CITY: Flourish for double bass
         choir (1960-61; Robert King Music; 6 min.)

         Commissioned by the American Wind Symphony
         Orchestra of Pennsylvania
         Dedicated to the American Wind Symphony
         Location of manuscript: Library of Congress,
         Washington D.C.

         Premiere

W163a.    1961 (4 July): London; the River Thames at Battersea; American Wind Symphony; Robert A. Boudreau, conductor.

W164.    THE HIGH SHERIFF'S FANFARE: For Two Trumpets (1963; Novello; 20 secs.)

> Written for Col. R.J. Longfield when he was High Sheriff of Dorset
> Location of manuscript: Lady Bliss, London

Premieres

W164a.    1963: Dorchester; Assize Court; Police Trumpeters

W164b.    1963 (24 August): Dorset; Lower Silton; Shaftsbury Silver Band

W165.    KENILWORTH: Suite for Brass Band (1936; R. Smith; 8 min.) See: B284

> Commissioned by the National Brass Band Championships of Great Britain
> Location of manuscript: Lady Bliss, London

Premiere

W165a.    1936 (26 September): London; Crystal Palace; used as the test piece in the 1936 Championships, the winning band being the Fodens Motor Works Band; Fred Mortimer, conductor. See: B144

Other selected performances

W165b.    1966 (12 March): Arnham; "Ons Genoegen" Hattem; Joap Stolp, conductor (Arrangement for Fanfare Band)

W166.    THE LINBURN AIR: March for Military Band (1964; Chappell; 4 min.)

> Dedicated to the Scottish National Institution for the War Blinded
> Location of manuscript: Unable to trace

Premiere

W166a.    1965 (14 November): Linburn; Band of the Gordon Highlanders; Colin Harper, conductor.

W167.    MUSIC FOR THE INVESTITURE OF THE PRINCE OF WALES: For Three Brass Choirs, each with Timpani and Percussion and Military Band (1968-69; unpublished; 8 min.)

> Commissioned by H.M. the Queen, through the Duke of Norfolk

Location of manuscript: Lady Bliss, London/RMSM, Kneller Hall

W167a. 1969 (1 July): Caernarfon; the Castle; Trumpeters of the RMSM, Kneller Hall; Lt. Col. C.H. Jaegar, conductor; State Trumpeters; Major W.G. Jackson, conductor; Band of the Welsh Fusiliers, H.C.R. Bentley conductor; BBC Welsh Orchestra, Wyn Morris, conductor. See: B36

W167b. 1970 (22 May): London; Royal Festival Hall; Trumpeters and Band of the RMSM, Kneller Hall; Lt. Col. C.H. Jaeger and T. Griffiths, conductors.

W168. MUSIC FOR A SERVICE OF THE ORDER OF THE BATH: For Three Trumpets, Two Trombones and Tuba (1956; unpublished; 1½ min.)

Location of manuscript: Lady Bliss, London

Premiere

W168a. 1956 (15 November): London; Westminster Abbey; Trumpeters of the Royal House Guards; Maj. J.E. Thirkle, conductor.

W169. MUSIC FOR THE WEDDING OF H.R.H. PRINCESS ALEXANDRA: For brass ensemble (1963; Novello; 4 min.)

Location of manuscript: Lady Bliss, London (part only)

Premiere

W169a. 1963 (24 April): London; Westminster Abbey; Trumpeters of the RMSM; Lt. Col. Basil H. Brown, conductor. See: B79

W170. MUSIC FOR THE WEDDING OF H.R.H. PRINCESS ANNE: For Brass Ensemble (1973; Novello; 3 min.)

Location of manuscript: Lady Bliss, London/Kneller Hall, Twickenham

Premiere

W170a. 1973 (14 November): London; Westminster Abbey; Trumpeters of the RMSM; Lt. Col. R.B. Bashford, conductor; Trumpeters of the Queen's Dragoon Guards; J.G. McColl, conductor.

W171. MUSIC FOR THE WEDDING OF H.R.H. PRINCESS MARGARET: For Brass Ensemble (1960; Novello; 3 min.)

Location of manuscript: RMSM, Kneller Hall/ Pierpont Morgan Library, New York

Premiere

W171a.  1960 (6 May); London; Westminster Abbey;
Trumpeters of the RMSM; Lt. Col. David McBain,
conductor. See: B46

W172.  PEACE FANFARE FOR CHILDREN: For Three Trumpets;
Three Trombones, Bells and Timpani (1944;
Novello, 39 secs).

Commissioned by the British Broadcasting
Corporation
Location of manuscript: Lady Bliss, London

Premiere

W172a.  1945 (8 May): London; Broadcasting House, BBC
Symphony Orchestra; Clarence Raybould,
conductor.

W173.  PRELUDE FOR BRASS, PERCUSSION, PICCOLO AND DOUBLE
BASSOON (1974; unpublished; 4½ min.)

Commissioned by Denis McCaldin, Professor of
Music, University of Lancaster
Location of manuscript: unable to trace

Premiere

W173a.  1974 (24 November): Lancaster; University of the
Main Hall; Lancaster Rehearsal Orchestra;
Denis McCaldin, conductor.

W174.  SALUTE TO LEHIGH UNIVERSITY: For Military Band
(1968; unpublished; 2 min.) Arranged by Jonathan
Elkus.

Commissioned by the Lehigh University Band
Dedicated to the Lehigh University Band
Location of manuscript: Lehigh University

Premieres

W174a.  1968 (14 September): Bethlehem, Pennsylvannia;
Taylor Stadium; Lehigh University Band; J.
Elkus, conductor.

W174b.  1968 (5 October): Lehigh University; Eugene
Gifford Grace Hall; Lehigh University Band
(the '97'); J. Elkus, conductor.

Other selected performances

W174c.  1978 (11 June): London; Embankment Gardens;
Marlboro' Brassers; Robert Peel, conductor.

W175.  SALUTE TO PAINTING: For Four Trumpets, Three
Trombones and Timpani (1954; Novello; 1 min.)

Dedicated to Sir Gerald Kelly on the occasion
of the Royal Academy Dinner, 28 April 1954
Location of manuscript: The Royal Academy of
Arts, London

Premiere

W175a.   1954 (28 April): London; Royal Academy of Arts,
         Piccadilly, Trumpeters of the Royal Artillery;
         Lt. Col. O.W. Geary, conductor. See: B43


W176.    SALUTE TO THE ROYAL SOCIETY: For Three Trumpets,
         Three Trombones, Timpani, Percussion and Organ
         (1960; World Library Publications; 6 min.)

         Written for the formal opening of the
         Tercentenary Celebrations of the Royal Society
         by H.M. the Queen
         Location of manuscript: Lady Bliss, London

         Premiere

W176a.   1960 (19 July): London; Royal Albert Hall;
         Trumpeters of the RMSM; George Thalben-Ball,
         organ; Arthur Bliss, conductor. See: B78

W177.    SALUTE TO SHALKESPEARE ON A PHRASE BY JOHN
         WILBYE: For Two Solo Trumpets, Three Trumpets,
         Three Trombones and Tuba (1964; Robert King
         Music; 1 min.)

         Written for the Argo recording A Homage to
         Shakespeare, issued in 1964 to mark the
         Shakespeare Quatercentenary
         Location of manuscript: Lady Bliss, London

         Premiere

W177a.   1964 (7 February): London, Decca Studios;
         Trumpeters of the RMSM, Kneller Hall; Lt. Col.
         Basil Brown, conductor.

         Other selected performances

W177b.   1973 (3 January): London; Royal Opera House,
         Covent Garden; Trumpeters of the RMSM, Kneller
         Hall; Lt. Col. Rodney Bashford, conductor.

W178.    SPIRIT OF THE AGE: For Brass Ensemble, Piano,
         Timpani and Percussion (1974; Robert King Music;
         2 min.)

         Commissioned by the British Broadcasting
         Corporation for a BBC2 series on British
         architecture, produced by John Drummond
         Location of manuscript: Lady Bliss, London

         Premiere

W178a.    1975 (11 January): London; BBC TV Centre, Lime
          Grove; members of the London Symphony
          Orchestra; Arthur Bliss, conductor.

W179.     THREE BACH CHORALES FROM THE ST. JOHN PASSION
          (J.S. BACH): Arranged for Three Trumpets, Three
          Trombones and Tuba (1960; unpublished; 3 min.)

          Location of manuscript: Lady Bliss, London

          Premiere

W179a.    1960 (6 September): Worcester; Cathedral Tower;
          Brass section of the City of Birmingham
          Symphony Orchestra; Melville Cook, conductor.

W180.     THREE JUBILANT AND THREE SOLEMN FANFARE: For
          Three Trumpets, Three Trombones and Tuba (1935;
          Novello; 2½min.)

          Commissioned by the British Broadcasting
          Corporation for a programme celebrating the
          Silver Jubilee of H.M. King George V
          Location of manuscript: unable to trace

          Premiere

W180a.    1935 (6 May): London; Broadcasting House; BBC
          Wireless Military Band; B. Walton O'Donnell,
          conductor. See: B37

          Other selected performances

W180b.    1945 (8 May): London; Broadcasting House; London
          Symphony Orchestra; Muir Mathieson, conductor
          (Arrangement for Orchestra).

W181.     TWO FANFARES FOR 'LET THE PEOPLE SING': For Three
          Trumpets, Three Trombones, Timpani and Percussion
          (1960; Novello; 30 secs.)

          Commissioned by the British Broadcasting
          Corporation
          Location of manuscript: Lady Bliss, London

          Premiere

W181a    1960 (28 June): London, Kingsway Hall; BBC Concert
          Orchestra; Arthur Bliss, conductor.


## PUBLISHING DIRECTORY

BOOSEY & HAWKES MUSIC PUBLISHING LTD.,295 Regent Street,
    London W1A 8JH. United States representative: Boosey &
    Hawkes Inc., P.O. Box 130 Oceanside, N.Y. 10572.

CAMBRIDGE UNIVERSITY PRESS, The Edinburgh Building,
    Shaftesbury Road, Cambridge CB2 2RU.

CHAPPELL MUSIC LTD., 50 New Bond Street, London W1A 2BR.
United States representative: Chappell Music Co., 810
Seventh Ave., New York, N.Y. 10019.

J.&W. CHESTER, LTD., 7-9 Eagle Court, London EC1M 5QD. United
States representative: Magnamusic-Baton, Inc., 10370 Page
Industrial Blvd., St. Louis, Missouri, 63132.

COMPOSERS' MUSIC CORP. - no longer extant.

J. CURWEN & SONS LTD. - now divided between Faber Music Ltd.
and G. Schirmer Ltd.

EMI MUSIC PUBLISHING LTD., 138-140 Charing Cross Road, London
WC2H 0LB.

FABER MUSIC LTD., 3 Queen Square, London WC1N 3AU.

F. & B. GOODWIN - no longer extant.

GOODWIN & TABB LTD. - no longer extant.

GOULD - no longer extant.

ROBERT KING MUSIC CO., 7 Canton Street, North Easton, Mass.
12356.

MOLENAAR MUZIEKCENTRALE Nv, Industrieweg 23, 19 Wormerveer,
Holland.

NOVELLO & CO LTD., 1-3 Upper James Street, London W1R 4BP.
United States representative: Theodore Presser Co.,
Presser Place, Bryn Mawr, Pennsylvania, 19010.

OXFORD UNIVERSITY PRESS LTD., Music Department, Walton
Street, Oxford OX2 6DP.

W.PAXTON & CO LTD. - no longer extant.

K. PROWSE MUSIC PUBLISHING CO LTD. - no longer extant.

G.RICORDI & CO LTD., The Bury Church Street, Chesham, Bucks.
HP5 1JG.

G. SCHIRMER LTD., 61-61 Lincoln's Inn Fields, London WC2A
3XB. United States representative: G. Schirmer, 866 Third
Avenue, New York, N.Y. 10022.

R.A. SMITH & CO LTD., P.O. Box 210, Watford, Herts. WD2 4YG.

STAINER & BELL LTD., 82 High Road, East Finchley, London N2
9PW.

UNIVERSAL EDITION, 2/3 Fareham Street, London W1V 4DU.

WALTON MUSIC CORPORATION, 1901 Avenue of the Stars, Los
Angeles, California 90067.

J. WILLIAMS - no longer extant.

WORLD LIBRARY PUBLICATIONS, 2145, Central Parkway,
Cincinnati, Ohio 45214.

# Discography

This selected discography includes long playing records currently available or deleted, mono or stereo.

The "see" references, e.g. See: B294, identify citations in the "Bibliography" section.

D1.  ADAM ZERO - Orchestral Suite

Lyrita SRCS 47. 1971 Nos. 5,7 and 10
London Symphony Orchestra; Arthur Bliss, conductor.
See: B291

His Master's Voice ASD 3687. 1979. Nos 1-2,4-8,10-12,15-16
Royal Liverpool Philharmonic Orchestra; Vernon Handley, conductor. See: B338

D2.  AN AGE OF KINGS - Arrangement for Concert Band

Pye (Golden Hour) GH603. n.d.
Coldstream Guards Band; Trevor Sharpe, conductor.

D3.  AUBADE FOR A CORONATION MORNING

Columbia 33CX 1063. 1953.
Elsie Suddaby and Margaret Field-Hyde, sopranos; the Cambridge University Madrigal Society; Boris Ord, conductor.
See:B403

RCA (Gold Seal) GL 25062. 1977.
Exultate Singers; Garrett O'Brien, conductor.
See:B250

D4.  THE BALLADS OF THE FOUR SEASONS : No.2 only

Jupiter JEPOC - 33. 1963.
Dorothy Dorow, soprano; Susan Bradshaw, piano.
See: B251

D5.  THE BELMONT VARIATIONS

>      EMI (Studio Two) TWOX 1053.  1976.
>      GUS Band; Geoffrey Brand, conductor.
>      See: B339

D6.  BIRTHDAY    GREETINGS    TO    THE    CROYDON    SYMPHONY
ORCHESTRA/FANFARE FOR A COMING OF AGE

>      RCA (Red Seal) RL25081.  1977.
>      Locke Consort of Brass; James Stobart, conductor.
>      See: B222.

D7.  BIRTHDAY SONG FOR A ROYAL CHILD

>      Waverley ZLP 2072.   1966.
>      Glasgow Phoenix Choir; Peter Mooney, conductor.

D8.  BLISS: ONE STEP

>      Polydor Super  2383-391.   1976.
>      Richard Rodney Bennett, piano.
>      See: B283

D9.  CALL TO ADVENTURE

>      His Master's Voice  7eg 8866.   1964.
>      Royal Marines Band; Vivian Dunn, conductor.

D10. CEREMONIAL PRELUDE - Recording of the First Performance

>      His Master's Voice   ASD 2264.  1965.
>      New Philharmonia Orchestra; Simon Preston, organ;
>      Arthur Bliss, conductor.

D11. CHECKMATE - Orchestral Suite

>      World Record Club.  ST52.  1960.
>      Sinfonia of London; Arthur Bliss, conductor.
>      See: B34, B279, B359

>      His Master's Voice ASD 3687.  1979.
>      Royal  Liverpool  Philharmonia  Orchestra,  Vernon
>      Handley, conductor.
>      See: B338

D12. CHRISTOPHER COLUMBUS - Orchestral Suite

>      His Master's Voice  ASD 3797.  1979.
>      City  of  Birmingham  Symphony  Orchestra;  Marcus
>      Dodds, conductor.
>      See: B362

D13. A COLOUR SYMPHONY

>      Decca LXT  5170.  1956.
>      London Symphony Orchestra; Arthur Bliss, conductor.
>      See: B421

>      EMI ASD 3416.  1977.

Royal Philharmonic Orchestra; Charles Groves, conductor.
See: B422

D14. CONCERTO FOR PIANO AND ORCHESTRA IN B-FLAT

Nixa GP 1167. 1953.
Noel Mewton-Wood, piano; Utrecht Symphony Orchestra; Walter Goehr, conductor.
See: B403

His Master's Voice ASD 499. 1962.
Trevor Bernard, piano; Philharmonic Orchestra; Malcolm Sargent, conductor.
See: B292

Unicorn-Kanchana DKP 9006. 1981.
Philip Fowke, piano; Royal Liverpool Philharmonic Orchestra; David Atherton, conductor.
See: B282

D15. CONCERTO FOR TWO PIANOS AND ORCHESTRA

His Master's Voice ASD 2612. 1970.
Cyril Smith and Phyllis Sellick, pianos; City of Birmingham Symphony Orchestra; Malcolm Arnold, conductor. For full details, see W12.
See: B278

D16. CONCERTO FOR VIOLIN AND ORCHESTRA

Decca LXT 5166. 1956.
Alfredo Campoli, violin; London Philharmonic Orchestra; Arthur Bliss, conductor.
See: B423

D17. CONCERTO FOR VIOLONCELLO AND ORCHESTRA

His Master's Voice ASD 3342. 1977.
Arto Noras, cello; Bournemouth Symphony Orchestra; Paavo Barglund, conductor.
See: B340

D18. CONVERSATIONS

Hyperion A66137. 1985.
Nash Ensemble; Lionel Friend, conductor.
See: B342

D19. DISCOURSE FOR ORCHESTRA

His Master's Voice ASD 3878. 1980.
City of Birmingham Symphony Orchestra; Vernon Handley, conductor.
See: B281

D20. EDINBURGH: Overture for Orchestra

His Master's Voice ASD 3878. 1980.

City of Birmingham Symphony Orchestra; Vernon Handley, conductor.
See: B281

D21. <u>FANFARE FOR THE COMMONWEALTH ARTS FESTIVAL/FANFARE FOR THE LORD MAYOR OF LONDON</u>

RCA (Red Seal) RL 25081. 1977.
Locke Consort of Brass; James Stobart, conductor.
See: B222

D22. <u>FANFARE FOR A DIGNIFIED OCCASION</u>

RCA (Red Seal) RL 25081. 1977.
Locke Consort of Brass; James Stobart, conductor.
See: B222

D23. <u>FANFARE FOR HEROES</u>

RCA (Red Seal) RL 25081. 1977.
Locke Consort of Brass; James Stobart, conductor.
See: B222

D24. <u>THE FIRST GUARDS</u>

Decca dfe 6499. n.d.
Band of the Grenadier Guards; -?- Harris, conductor.

D25. <u>GOD SAVE THE QUEEN</u>

Classics for Pleasure (EMI) CFP 198. 1972.
Royal Choral Society; London Philharmonic Orchestra; Arthur Bliss, conductor.

D26. <u>GREETINGS TO A CITY</u>

Decca (Ace of Diamonds) SDD 274. 1971.
Philip Jones Brass Ensemble.
See: B341

D27. <u>HYMN TO APOLLO</u>

Lyrita SRCS 55. 1971.
London Symphony Orchestra; Arthur Bliss, conductor.
See: B405

D28. <u>INTRODUCTION AND ALLEGRO</u>

Decca LXT 5170. 1956.
London Symphony Orchestra; Arthur Bliss, conductor.
See: B421

D29. <u>KENILWORTH</u>: Suite for Brass Band

EMI (Studio Two) TWOX 1053. 1976.
GUS Band; Geoffrey Brand, conductor.
See: B339

D30. <u>A KNOT OF RIDDLES</u>

Pye Virtuoso TPLS 13036. 1970.
John Shirley-Quirk, baritone; London Chamber
Orchestra; Wyn Morris, conductor.
See: B406

D31. THE LINBURN AIR

Decca SKL 4828. 1966.
Royal Highland Fusiliers Band.

D32. MADAME NOY

Hyperion A66137. 1985.
Elizabeth Gale, soprano; Nash Ensemble; Lionel
Friend, conductor.
See: B342

D33. MARCH OF HOMAGE IN HONOUR OF A GREAT MAN

Unicorn-Kanchana DKP 9006. 1981.
Royal Liverpool Philharmonic Orchestra; David
Atherton, conductor.
See: B282

D34. MEDITATIONS ON A THEME BY JOHN BLOW

Lyrita SRCS 33. 1966.
City of Birmingham Symphony Orchestra; Hugo
Rignold, conductor.
See: B280

His Master's Voice ASD 3878. 1980.
City of Birmingham Symphony Orchestra; Vernon
Handley, conductor.
See: B281

D35. MELEE FANTASQUE

Lyrita SRCS 50. 1971.
London Symphony Orchestra; Arthur Bliss, conductor.
See: B293

D36. MEMORIAL CONCERT

Decca LXT 5166. 1956.
Alfredo Campoli, violin; London Philharmonic
Orchestra; Arthur Bliss, conductor.
See: B423

D37. MIRACLE IN THE GORBALS - Orchestral Suite

Columbia 33CX 1205. 1955. Nos. 1-3,7-10,12 and 15
Philharmonia Orchestra; Arthur Bliss, conductor.
See: B294

EMI ASD 3342. 1977. Nos. 1-4,7-10,12 and 15
Bournemouth Symphony Orchestra; Paavo Berglund,
conductor.
See: B340

D38. <u>MORNING HEROES</u>

> His Master's Voice  SAN 365.  1975.
> John  Westbrook,  orator;  Liverpool  Philharmonic
> Choir;  Royal  Liverpool  Philharmonic  Orchestra;
> Charles Groves, conductor.
> <u>See</u>: B377

D39. <u>MUSIC FOR THE INVESTITURE OF H.R.H. THE PRINCE OF WALES</u>

> Delysee  SROY 1.  1969.
> Soundtrack of the proceedings at Caernafon Castle.
> <u>See</u>: B450

D40. <u>MUSIC FOR STRINGS</u>

> Columbia  33CX  1205.  1955.
> Philharmonic Orchestra; Arthur Bliss, conductor.
> <u>See</u>: B294

> Lyrita  SRCS 33.  1966.
> City  of  Birmingham  Symphony  Orchestra;  Hugo
> Rignold, conductor.
> <u>See</u>: B280

D41. <u>MUSIC FOR THE WEDDING OF H.R.H. PRINCESS ALEXANDRA</u>

> RCA (Red Seal) RL 25081.  1977.
> Locke Consort of Brass; James Stobart, conductor.
> <u>See</u>: B222

D42. <u>MUSIC FOR THE WEDDING OF H.R.H. PRINCESS ANNE</u>

> BBC  REW  163.  1973.
> Soundtrack of the proceedings in Westminster Abbey.

D43. <u>MUSIC FOR THE WEDDING OF H.R.H. PRINCESS MARGARET</u>

> RCA (Red Seal)  RL 25081.  1977
> Locke Consort of Brass; James Stobart, conductor.
> <u>See</u>: B222

D44. <u>PASTORAL: LIE STREWN THE WHITE FLOCKS</u>

> Pye Virtuoso  TPLS 13036.  1970.
> Sybil  Michelow,  mezzo-soprano;  Norman  Knight,
> flute;  Bruckner-Mahler  Choir  of  London;  London
> Chamber Orchestra; Wyn Morris, conductor.
> <u>See</u>: B406

> Hyperion A66175.  1985.
> Shirley Minty, mezzo-soprano; Judith Pearce, flute;
> Holst  Singers  and  Orchestra;  Hilary  Davan Wetton,
> conductor.
> <u>See</u>: B343

D45. <u>PRAELUDIUM</u>

> Wealden Prestige  WS206.  1981.

Christopher   Rathbone;   Paul   Chalkin   and   Giles
Vallis, percussion.
See: B397

D46. A PRAYER TO THE INFANT JESUS

Pilgrim  KLPS 42.   n.d.
Orpington   Junior   Singers;   Sheila   Mossman,
conductor.

Lyrita  SRCS 55.  1971.
Ambrosian Singers; Philip Ledger, conductor.
See: B405.

D47. PROCESSIONAL

His Master's Voice  ASD 3341.  1977.
Royal  Liverpool  Philharmonic  Orchestra;  Charles
Groves, conductor.
See: B363

CRD Vista   VPS 1055.   1977.  (Organ arrangement)
Timothy Farrell, organ
See: B444

D48. QUARTET [No.3]

Hyperion A66178.  1985.
Delme String Quartet.
See: B373

D49. QUARTET [No.4]

Decca  LX3038.  1951.
Griller String Quartet.
See: B408

Hyperion A66178.  1985.
Delme String Quartet
See: B373

D50. QUINTET FOR CLARINET AND STRINGS

World Record Club.  SCM 42.  1963.
Gervayse de Peyer, clarinet.  Melos Ensemble.
See: B409

D51. QUINTET FOR OBOE AND STRINGS

World Record Club  SCM 42.  1963.
Melos Ensemble
See: B409

Hyperion A66137.  1985.
Nash Ensemble; Lionel Friend, conductor.
See: B342

D52. RHAPSODY

Hyperion A66137.  1985.

Elizabeth Gale, soprano; Nash Ensemble; Lionel Friend, conductor.
See: B342

D53. RICH OR POOR

His Master's Voice CSD 3587. 1967.
Frederick Harvey, baritone; Gerald Moore, piano.
See: B252

D54. ROUT

Lyrita SRCS 55. 1971.
Rae Woodland, soprano; London Symphony Orchestra; Arthur Bliss, conductor.
See: B405

Hyperion A66137. 1985.
Elizabeth Gale, soprano; Nash Ensemble, Lionel Friend, conductor.
See: B342

D55. THE ROUT TROT

Polydor Super 2383-391. 1976.
Richard Rodney Bennett, piano.
See: B283

D56. THE ROYAL PALACES OF GREAT BRITAIN - Arrangement for Concert Band

Phillips S6308 048. 1971.
Band of H.M. Royal Marines; Cpt. L.T. Lambert, conductor

D57. SALUTE TO THE ROYAL SOCIETY

Sound News SM 122. 1979.
Trumpets of the RMSM; W. Lloyd Weber, organ; Trevor Sharpe, conductor.

D58. SALUE TO SHAKESPEARE

Argo ZNF 4. 1964.
Trumpets of the RMSM; Lt. Col. Basil Brown, conductor.

RCA (Red Seal) RL 25081. 1977.
Locke Consort of Brass; James Stobart, conductor.
See: B222

D59. SERENADE

Lyrita SRCS 55. 1971.
John Shirley Quirk, baritone; London Symphony Orchestra; Brian Priestman, conductor.
See: B405

D60. SET OF ACT TUNES AND DANCES

World Record Club   ST52.   1960.
Sinfonia of London; Arthur Bliss, conductor.
See: B34, B359

D61. SONATA FOR PIANO

Argo ZRG  786.  1975.
Rhonda Gillespie, piano.
See: B446

D62. SONATA FOR VIOLA AND PIANO

Delta DEL 12028.  1964.
Herbert Downes, viola; Leonard Cassini, piano.
See: B253

D63. THINGS TO COME - Orchestral Suites

RCA Victor  SB 2026.  1959.  Nos 2-4, 6-8
London Symphony Orchestra; Arthur Bliss, conductor.
See: B295

Decca (Phase Four) PFS 4363.  1976 Nos.1,7,8-10
National Philharmonic Orchestra; Bernard Herrmann,
conductor.
See: B424

EMI ASD 3416.  1977.  Suite - arr. Christopher
Palmer
Royal  Philharmonic  Orchestra;  Charles  Groves,
conductor.
See: B422

D64. THREE JUBILANT AND THREE SOLOMN FANFARES

Guild GRSP 701.  1977.  (No. 1 only)
Trumpeters  of  the  RMSM;  Cpt.  Trevor  Sharpe,
conductor.

D65. TULIPS

Poplets CP 2600.  n.d.
Barry  Alexander,  singer;  n.d.  with  guitar
accompaniment.

D66. WELCOME THE QUEEN

Columbia  DX 1912.  1954.
Philharmonic Orchestra; Arthur Bliss, conductor
See: B296

RCA Victor SB 2026.  1959
London Symphony Orchestra; Arthur Bliss, conductor
See: B295

Unicorn -Kanchana  DKP 9006.  1981.
Royal  Liverpool  Philharmonic  Orchestra;  David
Atherton, conductor.
See: B282

D67. THE WOMEN OF YUEH

       Hyperion A66137.   1985.
       Elizabeth  Gale,   soprano;   Nash   Ensemble;   Lionel
       Friend, conductor.
       See: B342

D68. THE WORLD IS CHARGED

       Lyrita  SRCS 55.   1971.
       Ambrosian   Singers;   London   Symphony   Orchestra;
       Philip Ledger, conductor.
       See: B405

# Bibliography

See" references refer to individual works and particular performances of those works as described in the "Works and Performances" section (e.g. <u>See</u> : W141b) and in the "Discography" (e.g., <u>See</u>: D64).

B1. Aber, Adolf. "Checkmate." <u>The Musical Times</u>, 78 (July 1937), pp.648-9.

> A detailed description of <u>Checkmate</u> after its first performance in Paris, the "combination of the two fundamental elements of the work, dramatic pantomime and splendid pageantry, giv(ing) a vivid impression of Bliss's power of design and the wealth of his musical palette." <u>See</u>: W5a

B2. Acton, Charles. "Bliss an original and personal composer." <u>The Irish Times</u> (Dublin), 28-29 March 1975, p.18.

> An obituary, pointing out that "as a composer, Bliss remain(ed) an original and very personal one, romantic but economical, English but of Gallic clarity, a disciple of the interwar Stravinsky, but always in debt to Stanford and Elgar."

B3. Anon. "Aeolian Hall." <u>The Daily Telegraph</u> (London), 26 June 1915, p.6.

> A review of a concert at the Aeolian Hall by the newly-formed Philharmonic String Quartet who played a <u>Quartet in A</u> by Arthur Bliss, a young writer whose music "... contains already much that is good and the promise of still better things to come." <u>See</u>: W51d

B4. Anon. "Aeolian Hall." <u>The Pall Mall and Globe</u> (London), 21 April 1921, p.9.

A review of an Edward Clark concert of English and French music. "Bliss's <u>Conversations</u> for several instruments were the best thing in this part of the programme, though it may be an offence against hospitality to say so." <u>See</u>: W37a

B5.  Anon. "An Adventurous Composer." <u>The Times</u> (London), 29 July 1961, p.4.

An article about Bliss's life, prompted by his 70th birthday. "Sir Arthur's career has, one feels, been one in musical terms unusually adventurous." Mention is also made of his conducting skills, "... Sir Arthur's devotion ... to composing has robbed the concert hall of a conductor of wide sympathies, vivid imagination and great authority ...."

B6.  Anon. "Arthur Bliss." <u>Tempo</u>, no.3 (May 1939), p.3.

A brief note indicating "... some idea of Bliss's musical versatility" and concluding with a mention of his latest work at that time, the <u>Concerto for Piano and Orchestra</u>.

B7.  Anon. "Arthur Bliss's New Quartet." <u>The Times</u> (London), 29 May 1942, p.6.

Mention of an early performance of the B-flat <u>String Quartet.</u> "Like all Bliss's work, it is intellectually well founded and vigorous.... Bliss writes good athletic prose ... and conducts an argument with skill."

B8.  Anon. "BBC's Bliss." <u>Evening Standard</u> (London) 1 April 1942, p.2.

A description of Arthur Bliss "... who succeeds Sir Adrian Boult as Director of Music for the BBC ...."

B9.  Anon. "BBC Concert: Bliss's new violin concerto." <u>The Times</u> (London), 12 May 1955, p.5.

A review of the BBC concert when Bliss's <u>Violin Concerto</u> was given its first performance by Alfredo Campoli. "The new work ... will be welcomed by violinists for it abounds in brilliant passages and lyrical melody, in generous solo sonority and exhilarating leggiero effects. The ideas are purposeful and fertile; all of them are not immediately striking, but they are entirely characteristic, and apt to their context." <u>See</u>:W13a

B10. Anon. "BBC Concert: Bliss's new work." <u>The Times</u> (London), 28 November 1935, p.12.

Mention of an early performance of Bliss's <u>Music for Strings</u>. "In so far as it reflects the thought of a vigorous mind it is a successful work."

B11.  Anon.  "BBC Radio Services to close down for 30 min."  The
      Times (London), 28 January 1965, p.6.

           Details about the arrangements for the funeral of
           Sir Winston Churchil on Saturday 30 January 1965.
           "A March of Homage in honour of a Great Man,
           composed by Sir Arthur Bliss, Master of the Queen's
           Music, is to be broadcast for the first time on
           Saturday just before the coverage of the funeral
           ceremony begins at 9.30 a.m. on the BBC Third
           network."  See W21a.

B12.  Anon.  "BBC Symphonic Concert: Morning Heroes."   The
      Times (London), 26 March 1931, p.12.

           A review of the first London performance of Morning
           Heroes, given by the National Chorus and BBC
           Symphony Orchestra.  See: W84b

B13.  Anon.  "The Beatitudes."  The Times (London), 26 May 1962,
      p.4.

           Description of the premiere of Bliss's cantata, The
           Beatitudes, given as part of the celebrations to
           mark the reconsecretion of Coventry Cathedral.  See:
           W75a

B14.  Anon.  "Bliss's Colour Symphony."  The Times (London),12
      March 1923, p.15.

           A report of the first Queen's Hall performance of
           Bliss's Colour Symphony which made a strong
           impression.  "Moreover, this was quite the most
           finished performance of the three yet heard."  See:
           W10b

B15.  Anon.  "Bliss's Edinburgh Overture."  The Times (London),
      22 August 1956, p.4.

           A review of the concert when Bliss conducted his
           overture Edinburgh.  "The new overture is a piece
           d'occasion constructed of various musical emblems
           of Scotland - the rhythm of the word "Edinburgh", a
           psalm tune and a strathspey.  These are strung
           together as a pot-pouri, with a slower section in
           the middle to commemorate Mary, Queen of Scots."
           See: W16a

B16.  Anon.  "A Bliss First Performance."  The Times (London),
      6 December 1955, p.3.

           An  announcement  giving  details  about  "the
           forthcoming  first  performance  of  Bliss's
           Meditations on a Theme by John Blow by the CBSO,
           conducted by Rudolf Schwarz."

B17.  Anon.  "Bliss's New Ballet."  The Times (London), 13
      December 1957, p.3.

A brief mention that "Sir Arthur Bliss has completed a new one-act ballet on the subject of The Lady of Shalott."

B18. Anon. "British Chamber Music." The Times (London), 26 June 1915, p.11.

A review of the concert at which Bliss's String Quartet was first performed. "It is in the bright key of A major and is made up of graceful themes which in their development emphasize instead of obliterate the natural brightness of the key." See: W51d

B19. Anon. "British Music." The Daily Telegraph (London), 13 June 1921, p.4.

An account of a concert given a the Wigmore Hall when "... Mr. Arthur Bliss's Concerto for pianoforte and tenor voice [was first performed]. The immediate success of this will long be remembered, for the applause was so insistent that the whole work had to be repeated." See: W12a

B20. Anon. "Checkmate : a new ballet by Arthur Bliss." The, Musical Times 78 (June 1937), pp.522-3.

A detailed examination of Checkmate, and an introduction to its scenario and music.

B21. Anon. "Concerto Coolidge." Gazzetta di Venezia, 12 September 1927, p.5.

Review of the Venetian premiere of Bliss's Oboe Quartet in a "concerto di musiche moderne offerto da Mrs. Elizabeth Coolidge al pubblico veneziano si e avolto jersera nella sala maggiore del conservatorio << Benedetto Marcello>> devanti ad un pubblico bellissimo per eleganza e per numero. ["concerto of modern music, offered to the Venetian public by Mrs Elizabeth Coolidge, (which) took place last night in the great hall of the conservatoire "Benedetto Marcello," in the presence of the public distinguished by its elegance and numbers."] See:W56a

B22. Anon. "Contemporary Music Centre." The Times (London), 22 January 1927, p.10.

Mention of a concert given by the Contemporary Music Centre at the Court House, Marylebone Lane, London. "The clarinet was played by Mr. Frederick Thurston who ... played four little solos,... one by Arthur Bliss." See: W34a

B23. Anon. "Contemporary Music Centre." The Times (London), 18 March 1932, p.12.

"The Joyce Book, a cycle of 13 songs from Pomes Penyeach by 13 contemporary composers, was sung at

the concert ... on Wednesday night .... Arthur
Bliss was almost romantic in *Simples* ...."
See:W121a

B24.  Anon. "Couples share wedding memories with Queen and
Duke." *The Times* (London), 21 November 1972, p.17.

A report about the Queen and Duke of Edinburgh
being joined, at their invitation, by nearly a
hundred couples in a simple thanksgiving service at
Westminster Abbey... to celebrate their twenty-
fifth wedding anniversary. See: W93a

B25.  Anon. "Covent Garden: Arthur Bliss's New Ballet." *The
Times* (London), 11 April 1946, p.6.

A detailed review of *Adam Zero* and its successful
premiere. "Such success in a difficult medium
could not have been achieved without music as
expressive, concise, and, in the best sense,
theatrical as Arthur Bliss's score, of which the
orchestra gave a brilliant performance." See: W4a

B26.  Anon. "Edinburgh Festival." *The Times* (London), 2
September 1950, p.8.

"Bliss's new string quartet was played for the
first time by the Griller Quartet.... It showed
ample invention and contained many happy ideas....
" See:W54a

B27.  Anon. "The Enchantress." *The Times* (London), 7 April
1952, p.3.

An account of the first public performance of *The
Enchantress* by Kathleen Ferrier at the Royal
Festival Hall. See: W78b

B28.  Anon. "Faure Centenary." *The Times* (London), 24 May
1945, p.8.

"Bliss's new march, which opened the concert, is at
the opposite pole, vigorous in his
characteristically athletic style, celebrating the
resurgence of France with trumpets playing and
flags flying." See: W26b

B29.  Anon. "Festival Hall: National Youth Orchestra." *The
Times* (London), 23 April 1945, p.10.

"Once again these talented school children showed
themselves able to challenge professional standards
in a programme which included ... "Birthday
Greetings to Her Majesty" specially composed for
the occasion by Sir Arthur Bliss...." See: W9a

B30.  Anon. "Film of a disaster at sea and its sequel." *The
Times* (London), 11 March 1957, p.5.

A review of the film <u>Seven Waves Away</u> which "... has honesty of a sort and courage, and it brings the best out of that ... marvellous actor, Mr. Tyrone Power." <u>See</u>: W138a

B31. Anon. "Forces to Inspire BBC Music." <u>News Chronicle</u> (London), 2 April 1942, p.3.

"Arthur Bliss, the composer, who yesterday took over from Sir Adrian Boult as Director of Music at the BBC, is not satisfied with the present policy of broadcasting music. He has many ideas for improvements, and he has the enthusiasm needful for carrying out his ideas. Mr. Bliss's plans embrace all forms of music, from swing to symphony."

B32. Anon. "The French Six." <u>The Times</u> (London), 21 April 1921, p.13.

An account of the concert when Bliss's <u>Conversations</u> were performed. "The first movement ... is laughable, and its second ... is musical ...." <u>See</u>: W37a

B33. Anon. "From 'Colour' Symphony to Charlie Chaplin." <u>The Musical Mirror</u> (London), April 1923, p.104.

A brief interview with Bliss before his departure for America, which includes mention of his intention to open negotiations with Charles Chaplin in Los Angeles. "He would make an excellent subject for musical treatment."

B34. Anon. "The Greatest Record We Have Ever Issued." <u>Record Review</u> (London), 4 (July 1960), p.2.

An interesting account of the background to the recording (World Record Club ST52), made by Bliss and the Sinfonia of London. <u>See</u>: D11, D60

B35. Anon. "Helping British Music." <u>The Times</u> (London), 19 May 1921, p.8.

An announcement that the trustees of the Carnegie United Kingdom Trust ... have selected five compositions for publication, including <u>Rhapsody for 2 voices, woodwind and strings</u> by Arthur Bliss. This composition is described as "a delicate and sensitive piece of work with great melodic charm and a pure and classical sense of beauty." <u>See</u>: W116

B36. Anon. "Investiture of the Prince of Wales." <u>The Times</u> (London), 2 July 1969, p.1.

A description of the pomp and ceremonial accompanying the Investiture of the Prince of Wales by H.M. Queen Elizabeth II at Caernafon Castle. <u>See</u>: W167a

B37.  Anon.  "The King to his People."  <u>The Times</u> (London), 7
      May 1935, p.24.

      A report of the broadcast given in honour of the
      Silver Jubilee of King George V on 6 May 1935.
      <u>See</u>: W180a

B38.  Anon.  "The Kutcher Quartet."  <u>The Times</u> (London), 20
      February 1933, p.8.

      An account of the first public performance of
      Bliss's <u>Clarinet Quintet</u> by the Kutcher Quartet and
      Frederick Thurston, playing the clarinet.  "...
      Arthur Bliss seems definitely to have passed into a
      different phase of musical thought from that which
      dominated him when his work came conspicuously
      before the public 10 years or so ago.  ... the
      quintet is a valuable addition to the repertory of
      modern chamber music."  <u>See</u>: W55b

B39.  Anon.  "La Serva Padrona."  <u>The Times</u> (London), 31
      January 1919, p.11.

      A review of Pergolesi's opera, arranged by Arthur
      Bliss, given at the Lyric Theatre, Hammersmith,
      London. <u>See</u>: W1a

B40.  Anon.  "Lane Series Tuesday Features Britain's Royal
      Choral Society."  <u>Burlington Free Press</u>, 20 October
      1969, p.5.

      A report of a RCS concert at Burlington's Memorial
      Auditorium.  "<u>The Star Spangled Banner</u> and <u>God Save
      the Queen</u> will be sung at the opening of the
      concert."  <u>See</u>: W79a

B41.  Anon.  "Last Night's Music."  <u>The Standard</u> (London), 26
      June 1915, p.8.

      An account of the Philharmonic String Quartet
      concert at the Aeolian Hall, London.  Arthur
      Bliss's <u>Quartet in A major</u> is described as a "work
      of sound musicianship" and "the Andante Sostenuto
      ... making a good impression." <u>See</u>: W51d

B42.  Anon.  "Llandaff Service of Thanksgiving."  <u>The Times</u>
      (London), 8 August 1960, p.10.

      A description of the service of thanksgiving in
      Llandaff Cathedral (South Wales), marking the
      restoration of the Cathedral which was severely
      damaged in a 1941 air raid.  <u>See</u>: W101a

B43.  Anon.  "Loan of Pictures."  <u>The Times</u> (London), 29 April
      1954, p.3.

      An account of the annual banquet of the Royal
      Academy of Burlington House."  During the evening,
      <u>Salute to Painting</u>, composed for the occasion by
      Sir Arthur Bliss, Master of the Queen's Music, was

played.   It was performed by herald trumpeters of
the Royal Artillery before the president [Sir
Gerald Kelly] proposed the toast "British Music,"
to which Sir Arthur Bliss replied."  See:W175a

B44. Anon. "Mary of Magdala."  The Times (London),4 September
     1963, p.13.

     A report of the first performance of Mary of
     Magdala given in Worcester Cathedral, as part of
     the 1963 Three-Choirs Festival.  See: W83a

B45. Anon.  "Master of the Queen's Music."  The Times
     (London), 18 November 1953, p.8.

     The official announcement, taken from the London
     Gazette, that "Sir Arthur Bliss has been appointed
     Master of the Music to her Majesty, in succession
     to the late Sir Arnold Bax...."

B46. Anon.  "Memorable Close to Wedding Day [Princess
     Margaret]."  The Times (London), 7 May 1960, p.8.

     A detailed description of the wedding ceremony in
     Westminster Abbey when H.R.H. Princess Margaret
     married Anthony Armstrong-Jones.  See:W171a

B47. Anon.  "Memorial Services: Sir Arthur Bliss."  The Times
     (London), 21 May 1975, p.17.

     Details about and a list of people attending, the
     memorial service in Westminster Abbey for Sir
     Arthur Bliss.

B48. Anon.  "Miss Moger's Recital."  The Daily Telegraph
     (London), 28 January 1921, p.8.

     "The Thistles of Mr. Bliss... is a good example of
     the merry variety, and even if the relationship
     between music and text is at moments a little
     strained, it ends well."  See: W129b

B49. Anon.  "Miss Thursfield's Recital."  Westminster Gazette
     (London), 25 June 1920, p.5.

     A report of the first performance of Madam Noy, by
     Anne Thursfield, which is described as "less
     effective" than other items in the programme.  See:
     W115a

B50. Anon.  "Modern Chamber Music."  The Daily Telegraph
     (London), 21 April 1921, p.13.

     A review of the Edward Clark concert, at a crowded
     Aeolian Hall, which included Conversations.  "Some
     of this music is witty, some of it long-winded,
     some of it would easily bear repetition ...."  See:
     W37a

B51. Anon. "Morning Heroes." The New York Times, 8 October 1931, p.21.

Details about the American premiere of Morning Heroes at the Worcester Music Festival. See: W84c

B52. Anon. "Morning Heroes." The Times (London), 24 October 1930, p.12.

An account of the first performance of Bliss's choral symphony at the Norwich Festival. "...we realize that Arthur Bliss had made his great step forward and, in saying what is old, has said something new and true." See: W84a

B53. Anon. "Music : A Chamber Orchestra." The Times (London) 28 April 1920, p.14.

A report of the concert when Bliss's Quintet for Piano and Strings was given its first performance. It is described as "... an exceedingly interesting work rising to moments of striking beauty in the central movement of the three." See: W57b

B54. Anon. "Music that demands choreography." The Times (London), 29 September 1965, p.14.

A review of the first performance of the revised version Discourse for Orchestra." ... Sir Arthur has had quite a lot of second thoughts, and the revised score ... includes cuts, readjustments and a larger orchestra." See: W15b

B55. Anon. "A Musical 'Rout'." The Times (London), 17 December 1920, p.10.

"At a chamber concert given at 139 Piccadilly ..., a new work called Rout, by Mr. Arthur Bliss, was given a first performance.... it is exceedingly clever, and proved quite captivating .... See: W118a

B56. Anon. "Musicians' Tribute to Sir Henry Wood." The Times (London), 25 March 1944, p.6.

A description of the proceedings, held at the Savoy Hotel, London, to celebrate the 75th birthday of Henry Wood. "...and a Fanfare specially composed by Mr. Arthur Bliss was performed by trumpeters of the Royal Military School of Music." See: W160a

B57. Anon. "National Brass Band Championships." The Times (London), 21 October 1963, p.7.

A report about the 1963 National Brass Band Championships, held in the Royal Albert Hall, when the Belmont Variations were used as the test piece. See: W149a

B58. Anon.   "The New Development in Music."  The Observer
       (London), 3 July 1921, p.7.

       Concerning Arthur Bliss's lecture, to the Society
       of Women Musicians, about"... composers who are in
       the    forefront    of    the    new    development    -    a
       development, which ... is continually striving at
       simplicity, sincerity, and vitality of expression."

B59. Anon.   "New  Orchestral  Work  by  Bliss."  The  Times
       (London), 15 December 1955, p.5.

       A review of the first performance of Meditations on
       a Theme by John Blow.  "The thematic structure
       though complex is taut, the individual Meditations
       are    richly    inventive,    the    interlude    has    the
       dramatic  quality  of  Bliss's  ballet  scores,  the
       unity  of  the  whole  is  trebly  secure  from  its
       literary  as  well  as  its  thematic  and  structure
       coherence.  Orchestrally  it  is  a  virtuoso  piece,
       for  Bliss  has  in  his  maturity  learned  how  to
       combine   the   romantic   grand   manner   with   the
       astringent  subject  matter  that  he  produced  as  a
       young man."  See: W22a

B60. Anon.  "New  Viola  Sonata."   The  Times  (London),  4
       November 1933, p.8.

       A  report  about  the  broadcast  by  Lionell  Tertis
       which  included  the  first  performance  of  Bliss's
       Viola  Sonata.   "It  is  a  work  of  high  interest  and
       considerable  beauty,  in  which  the  beauty  appears
       first and the interest deepens later."  See: W60b

B61. Anon. "Norwich Musical Festival: New choral symphony by
       Bliss." The Times (London), 23 October 1930, p.12.

       A  detailed  description  of  the  first  performance  of
       Morning  Heroes  at  the  1930  Norwich  Festival.  See:
       W84a

B62. Anon. "The Olympians." The Musical Times, 90 (September
       1949), pp.312-13.

       Extended  background  and  examination  of  Bliss's
       opera  The  Olympians,  first  performed  at  the  Royal
       Opera House, Covent Garden.  See: W2a

B63. Anon. "The Olympians." The Times (London), 30 September
       1949, p.6.

       A  report  concerning  the  first  performance  of  The
       Olympians  at  Covent  Garden,  with  some  discussion  of
       the opera.  See: W2a

B64. Anon. "Our Elgar Fugue Competition." The Music Student,
       IX (November 1916), p.108.

       Details  of  the  winners  of  the  Fugue  Competition,
       with mention of" ... a delightful fugue for string

quartet by Captain Arthur Bliss (London)." The text of a letter from Bliss is also printed. <u>See</u>: W39

B65. Anon. "Profile : Sir Arthur Bliss." <u>The Observer</u> (London), 29 November 1953, p.3.

A general article about Bliss and his career, written at the time of his appointment to the post of Master of the Queen's Music.

B66. Anon. "Promenade concert: Bliss and Britten." <u>The Times</u> (London), 18 August, 1939, p.8.

Description of the first London (and United Kingdom) performance of Arthur Bliss's <u>Piano Concerto</u>, commissioned for the 1939 New York World Fair. <u>See</u>: W11b

B67. Anon. "Promenade Concert : British Composers' Works." <u>The Times</u> (London), 6 September 1929, p.10.

A review of the concert which included Arthur Bliss's <u>Concerto for Two Pianos</u> "... which is a re-writing of the earlier concerto for piano and tenor voice (which) uses the character of the piano, especially its percussive character, as the foundation for its thematic ideas, which are pointed ones. The whole work (in one movement) is pithy; the influence of Stravinsky, which was at one time powerful with Bliss, has been absorbed and turned to good purpose to serve his own individuality. The work scored a success, and what is more, deserved it." <u>See</u>: W12c

B68. Anon. "Promenade Concert : Mr. Arthur Bliss's Melee Fantasque." <u>The Times</u> (London), 14 October 1921, p.8.

"... Mr. Bliss's <u>Melee Fantasque</u> (is) a most spirited work of some dimensions, dedicated to the memory of Claude Lovat Fraser. Mr. Bliss conducted and the performance was admirably clear." <u>See</u>: W23a

B69. Anon. "Promenade Concert: New work by Mr. Arthur Bliss." <u>The Times</u> (London), 9 September 1926, p.10.

"An <u>Introduction and Allegro</u> for full orchestra by Mr. Arthur Bliss was given its first performance ... last night. The new work shows a considerable development in Mr. Bliss's style. There is less attempt to dazzle, and a more serious outlook than he has hitherto shown. The <u>Introduction and Allegro</u> is straightforward, vigorous, and indeed, invigorating music." <u>See</u>: W20a

B70. Anon. "Promenade Concert: Two Symphonies." <u>The Times</u> (London), 5 October 1928, p.12.

An account of the Queen's Hall concert which
included the last movement of Arthur Bliss's Colour
Symphony [Pyanepsion].  "Bliss's music is clever
and appears to the intellect which can enjoy his
skilful weaving of the double fugue and his
decorations of it with orchestral and rhythmic
devices."  See: W10d

B71. Anon. "The Pursuit of Bliss."  The Morning Post
     (London), 31st December 1935, p.10.

     A leader describing the conclusions reached of
     Bliss's tour of Britain, carried out on behalf of
     the BBC.

B72. Anon. "Queen's Hall: BBC Symphony Concert."  The Times
     (London), 28 April 1932, p.12.

     A review of the performance of the revised version
     of the Colour Symphony."  It is all very skilful;
     some of it very beautiful...."  See:W10e

B73, Anon. "Recitals of the Week: Concerts Spirituels."  The
     Times (London), 5 February 1926, p.12.

     "A suite for pianoforte called Masks, by Arthur
     Bliss, was played by Mr. Arthur Benjamin
     brilliantly, and with a glittering hardness of tone
     which this music seems to demand."  See: W43a

B74. Anon. "Recitals of the Week: English and Italian Songs."
     The Times (London), 28 January 1921, p.8.

     "Another experiment in accompaniment was Arthur
     Bliss's The Thistles, with clarinet obligato (Mr.
     F.J. Thurston), which was more successful in
     performance than was Holst's work.  Whimsical and
     fanciful, with queer sounds in the clarinet part,
     Bliss seems to make his point ... without letting
     his hearers into the secret of how he does it."
     See:W129b

B75. Anon. "Recitals of the Week: Miss Elizabeth Nicol."  The
     Times (London), 9 October 1925, p.12.

     Mention of the first performance, by Elizabeth
     Nicol, of The Fallow Deer at the Lonely House - " a
     pianoforte piece with voice obligato."  See: W111a

B76. Anon. "Recital of the Week : Miss Sybil Scanes and Mr.
     Paul Belinfante."  The Times (London), 8 April 1927,
     p.12.

     A review of the joint recital which included "...
     three songs and a 'vocalize' for voice and violin
     by Mr. Arthur Bliss....  The vocalise sounded like
     an accompanied cadenza....  Of the songs, The Mad
     Woman of Punnetstown was perhaps the best, though
     Sea Love would doubtless sound better if taken less
     dramatically."  See W112a

B77. Anon. "Royal Philharmonic Society." The Times (London),
28 January 1927, p.12.

"In the middle of the programme there was a new
symphonic poem called Hymn to Apollo, by Arthur
Bliss.... He has changed a good deal since the
days when he entertained us with Rout and the like.
On the whole... it seemed to us interesting and
finely thought, rather than felt, music, with a
tone of voice of its own, and a continuity of
design which made it easy to follow." See: W19b

B78. Anon. "Royal Society Host to Great International
Gathering." The Times (London), 20 July 1960, p.5.

A report of the opening ceremony of the
tercentenary celebrations of the Royal Society. "A
Salute in music came from Sir Arthur Bliss, Master
of the Queen's Musick, who conducted it." See:
W176a

B79. Anon. "Royal Wedding Ceremony of Impressive Smoothness
[Princess Alexandra]." The Times (London), 25 April,
1963, p.12.

A detailed account of the wedding service, in
Westminster Abbey, of Princess Alexandra of Kent
and Mr. Angus Ogilvy. See: W169a

B80. Anon. "Sadler's Wells Ballet: Checkmate." The Times
(London), 6 October 1937, p.12.

A review of the first London performance of
Checkmate. "The music has an enormous nervous
energy, which makes the battle almost terrifyingly
real. The ballet, which was conducted by Mr.
Constant Lambert, was most enthusiastically
received." See: W5b

B81. Anon. "St. Martin's Lane." The Times (London), 9
September 1949, p.2.

A review of Summer Day's Dream by J.B. Priestley,
together with a summary of the play's story-line.
See: W146b

B82. Anon. "Sadler's Wells Ballet." The Times (London), 27
October 1944, p.6.

An account of the first performance of Miracle in
the Gorbals, "... a new ballet... not lacking in
dramatic power. ... the honours of this discordant
ballet go to the composer, Arthur Bliss, who knows
how to handle discords." See: W8a

B83. Anon. "Saturday's Concerts: new concerto by Arthur
Bliss." The Times (London), 13 June 1921, p.8.

"A new concerto for piano and tenor voice was the
central work in the programme of music for chamber

orchestra which Mr. Arthur Bliss conducted at the Wigmore Hall.... ... whatever may be its defects, there is genuine music in this work. Apart from certain wilful excrescences of sound, the music moves through finely impulsive ideas with strong contrasts of mood and yet preserves identity by thematic development. It is substantial music, and it was received with what seemed like genuine enjoyment by the large audience." <u>See</u>: W12a

B84. Anon. "Savitri : Holst's unconventional opera." <u>The Times</u> (London), 24 June 1921, p.13.

An account of the first performance of Holst's opera, directed by Mr. Arthur Bliss.

B85. Anon. "Shostakovich's new cello concerto." <u>The Times</u> (London), 7 October 1966, p.7.

Mention of Sir Arthur Bliss handing the Royal Philharmonic Society's gold medal to the Soviet Ambassador (for Dimitri Shostakovich) at a concert in the Royal Festival Hall, London.

B86. Anon. "Sir Arthur Bliss." <u>The Scotsman</u> (Edinburgh), 28 March 1975, p.11.

An obituary describing Bliss's life work, with the emphasis on Edinburgh and Scotland.

B87. Anon. "Sir Arthur Bliss, 83, Composer, Master of Queen's Musick, Dies." <u>The New York Times</u>, 28 March 1975, p.30.

An obituary surveying Sir Arthur Bliss's life, career, work and music.

B88. Anon. "Sir Arthur Bliss, fogey to some, looking ahead." <u>Antelope Valley Ledger Gazette</u>, 19 September 1961, p.7.

"Sir Arthur, just turned 70, is deemed a fogey by some young men of music because of his work.... Yet Sir Arthur remains as forward looking as any of young men in music."

B89. Anon. "Sir Arthur Bliss, Master of the Queen's Musick." <u>The Washington Post</u>, 29 March 1975, Section B, p.4.

An obituary mentioning Bliss's work as Master of the Queen's Musick, together with his other output.

B90. Anon. "Sir Arthur Bliss: A Modern Romantic." <u>The Times</u> (London), 27 April 1956, p.3.

A lengthy article surveying Bliss's life, influences, and music which is described as "in tune with the English tradition."

B91. Anon. "Sir Arthur Bliss: Three Youth and Music Members talk to the Master of the Queen's Musick." <u>Youth and Music News</u>, November 1971, p.3.

A general interview highlighting what has inspired Sir Arthur Bliss, his views on electronic music, his own personal tastes in music and finally his routine for composition.

B92. Anon. "Splendid Pageantry Commemorates Abbey's 900th Anniversary." <u>The Times</u> (London), 29 December 1965, p.8.

A detailed description of the ceremony in Westminster Abbey, London, commemorating the 900th anniversary of it consecration. "Finally, with crash of cymbals and sound of trumpets, a <u>Ceremonial Prelude</u> composed for the occasion welcomed the entry of the Queen, the Duke of Edinburgh, the Prince of Wales and Princess Anne. The composer, Sir Arthur Bliss, Master of the Queen's Music, conducted from the organ loft." <u>See</u>: W152a

B93. Anon. "Thanksgiving for Royal Birth." <u>The Times</u> (London), 22 February 1960, p.10.

An account of the events surrounding the birth of Prince Andrew. "Mr. C. Day Lewis has written and Sir Arthur Bliss, Master of the Queen's Musick, has composed a <u>Birthday Song for a Royal Child</u>. It is described ... as somewhat analogous to the welcome odes composed by Henry Purcell, a former Master of the Queen's Musick, for various royal occasions." <u>See</u>: W76a

B94. Anon. "The Three Choirs Festival: New works by Bliss and Goossens." <u>The Times</u> (London), 8 September 1922, p.13.

A review of the concert which included the first performance of the <u>Colour Symphony</u>. "Bliss's symphony marks a new stage in his career, an important one, because the first thing which must impress everyone is its earnestness. Some time age it seemed an open question whether Bliss, with all his talents and facility, would develop as a serious composer, or be content to play with the resources of modern instrumental tone-colour and do little things for the astonishment of those who feed on astonishment. The Concerto seemed to me ... to show that he was out for the bigger thing; this Symphony leaves no doubt about it." <u>See</u>: W10a

B95. Anon. "Thursday Morning." <u>The Gloucester Journal</u>, 9 September 1922, p.9.

A detailed account of Bliss's <u>Colour Symphony</u> and its first performance in Gloucester Cathedral. <u>See</u>: W10a

B96. Anon. "Twenty-first Anniversary." <u>Action News</u> (London), 2 (January 1974),p.1.

A description of the service in St. Paul's Cathedral, held to mark the 21st Anniversary of Action Research for the Crippled Child, a charity with which Sir Arthur and Lady Bliss were closely involved. "The trumpeters of the Kneller Hall School of Music - their trumpets hung with banners of scarlet and gold - sounded the fanfare specially composed by Sir Arthur Bliss...." <u>See</u>: W157a

B97. Anon. "Twone, The House of Felicity." <u>The Times</u> (London), 17 March 1923, p.8.

"A suite for small orchestra followed a three themes - two diatonic... , and the third, a scale which was obviously set as a puzzle. At any rate, those of the five composers who alluded to it either treated it as an arpeggio or left it as meaningless as it appeared on the paper.... Arthur Bliss wrote a good poem to the subject...." <u>See</u>: W31a

B98. Anon. "The Week's Music: The French Six." <u>The Sunday Times</u> (London), 24 April 1921, p.6.

"By far the best of the new works was Mr. Bliss's <u>Conversations</u>. The superiority of Mr. Bliss's work comes from the fact that he is really a subtle and original harmonic thinking...." <u>See</u>:W37a

B99. Antcliffe, Herbert. "Arthur Bliss's new work in Amsterdam." <u>Musical News and Herald</u>, 11 December 1926, pp.518-9.

An account of the first performance of <u>Hymn to Apollo</u>, "... produced by the Amsterdam Concertebouw Orchestra, and its reception by the public was exceptionally cordial." <u>See</u>: W19a

B100.Aprahamian, Felix. "Sir Arthur Bliss - Master of the Queen's Music." <u>Crescendo</u>, no. 138, December 1964, p.67.

A detailed profile of Bliss, his life and music.

B101.Arundel, Denis. "Bliss's British Concert in Finland." <u>Music and Musicians</u>, November 1957, p.15.

A description of a concert in Helsinki devoted to British music and conducted by Bliss.

B102.Autolycus. "Unconsidered Trifles." <u>Musical Opinion</u>, September 1921, p.1002.

An account of Bliss's paper, given to the Society of Women Musicians, entitled 'What Modern Composition is aiming at.'

B103.B., P.A. "Festival Concerts." The Advertiser (Macclesfield), 20 May 1966, p.28.

" The Fanfare Prelude, specially written for the
occasion by the conductor ... opened the concert."
See: W4c

B104.Banfield, S.  "Sensibility and English Song: critical
studies of the Early 20th Century: Vol.2." Cambridge,
Cambridge       University       Press,       1985,
pp.322-4,365-370,421-3.

A detailed survey of Bliss's songs, showing him as
"... a traditionalist who took a long time to
settle down."

B105.Beaumont, C.W.   "The Sadler's Wells Ballet." London,
C.W. Beaumont, 1946, pp.117-122.

A general introduction to the ballet, Checkmate.
See: W5

B106.Beechey. G.   "Walter de la Mare: settings of his
poetry."  The Musical Times 114 (April 1973),
pp.371-3.

A centenary article about the poet Walter de la
Mare with brief reference to Bliss's setting of
Three Romantic Songs. See: W123

B107.Benthall, M., Dane, C., Middleton, M.H., Haskell, A.L.
and Blom, E. "Hamlet and Miracle in the Gorbals."
London. The Bodley Head, 1949, pp.26-44.

A very detailed introduction, with photographs from
the original production, to the ballet, Miracle in
the Gorbals. See: W8

B108.Bishop. J. "Bon Papa : an interview with Air Arthur
Bliss." Youth and Music News, July 1963, p.10.

A brief article about Bliss and his music, with
quotations from the composer.

B109.Bliss, Arthur. "Anxiety for the Author's Right."  The
Times (London), 16 June 1964, p.12.

The report of a speech by Bliss, delivered at the
Guildhall in London, inaugurating the Congress of
the International Confederation of Authors' and
Composers' Societies.

B110.Bliss, Arthur. "Arnold Bax: 1883-1953." Music and
Letters, XXXV (January 1954), p.1.

A contribution, by Bliss, to a set of reminiscences
about Arnold Bax who had died on 3 October 1953.

B111.Bliss, Arthur. "Arnold Schoenberg: 1874-1951." Music and
Letters, XXXII (October 1951), p.307.

A brief contribution to a set of essays about Arnold Schoenberg who had recently died.

B112. Bliss, Arthur. "Arthur Bliss's Morning Heroes". Monthly Musical Record, LX (1 October 1930), pp.289-291.

A brief account, movement by movement, of Morning Heroes by the composer, with musical examples. See: W84

B113. Bliss, Arthur. "As I Remember." London, Faber and Faber, 1970, 269 pp.

Bliss's enthralling autobiography, with illustrations, commenced in 1966 and dedicated to Trudy Bliss.

B114. Bliss, Arthur. "Aspects of Contemporary Music." The Musical Times, 75 (May 1934), pp. 401-5.

Extracts for Bliss's lectures on contemporary music, given to the Royal Institution on 8,15 and 22 March 1934.

B115. Bliss, Arthur. "BBC Programmes." The Times (London), 19 February 1958, p.9.

A letter to the Editor, signed by Bliss and others, about the effect of new changes in the BBC's new policies for sound broadcasting.

B116. Bliss, Arthur. "Mr. Bernard van Dieren." The Times (London), 25 April 1936, p.14.

An obituary of Bernard van Dieren, with an addition by Arthur Bliss who described him as a "composer of genius, master of critical analysis, sensitive craftsman in wood and leather, trained chemist, and accomplished linguist...."

B117. Bliss, Arthur. "Berners and Bax." The League of Composers Review (New York), 1 (February 1924), pp.26-7.

A short article about Gerald Berners and Arnold Bax who "... represent two extremes in English music."

B118. Bliss, Arthur. "British Composers." The Sunday Times (London), 24 October 1943, p.4.

A letter from Bliss, as the BBC's Director of Music, answering criticism that not enough British music was being broadcast.

B119. Bliss, Arthur. "British Light Music undervalued." The Times (London), 31 May 1960, p.4.

An appeal, by Bliss, for more use of British light popular music in programmes, made at the opening of

new offices in London of the Performing Right
Society.

B120.Bliss, Arthur. "British Musicians in Moscow." Voks
Bulletin (Moscow), No.6 (June 1956), pp.36-7.

An account of Bliss's visit to the Soviet Union,
accompanied by Clarence Raybould, Alfredo Campoli,
Cyril Smith, Phyllis Sellick, Gerald Moore, Leon
Goossens, Jenifer Vyvyan and Trudy Bliss.

B121.Bliss, Arthur. "Britten beats Strike." The Times
(London), 20 December 1969, p.1.

Arthur Bliss's views about the Musicians Union,
withdrawing its services at a particular concert.

B122.Bliss, Arthur. "Broadcast Music : Early Flowering and
Mature Growth." The Listener, XXI, 2 February 1939,
p.280.

A discussion concerning the very early work of
great composers, including Mozart and Mendelssohn,
and Arlecchino by Busoni.

B123.Bliss, Arthur. "Broadcast Music: French, Italian and
German." The Listener, XXI, 19 January 1939, p.172.

A review of the past week's broadcast music, with
the emphasis on Delibes and Mozart.

B124.Bliss, Arthur. "Broadcast Music: Mostly Brahms." The
Listener, XXI, 9 February 1939, p.332.

A discussion of several major works of Brahms which
had been played recently on the radio-including the
Third Symphony, the clarinet Quintet, a clarinet
Sonata and some songs.

B125.Bliss, Arthur. "Broadcast Music: Two Symphonies and Two
Sonatas." The Listener, XXI, 26 January 1939, p.228.

An account of symphonies by Magnard and Boughton
and sonatas, played by Philip Levi, of Busoni and
Szymanowski.

B126.Bliss, Arthur. "Chamber Music by Living Composers."
London. British Music Information Centre. 1969.

A forward to the chamber music catalogue, issued by
the BMIC which was established by The Composers'
Guild of Britain in 1967.

B127.Bliss, Arthur. "Children at risk." The Sunday Times
(London), 29 April 1973, p.19.

A letter prompted by "... the terrible case of the
murdered child, Maria Colwell."

B128.Bliss, Arthur. "Composers' Forum - subject: opera." Musical America 73 (February 1953), pp.33 and 152.

The answers to six questions about opera from seven distinguished composers, representatives of contemporary Europe, including Arthur Bliss from the United Kingdom.

B129.Bliss, Arthur. "Concerto for Violin and Orchestra (1955)". The Musical Times 96 (June 1955), pp.304-5.

An analysis, movement by movement with musical examples, of the Violin Concerto, completed at the beginning of 1955. See:W13

B130.Bliss, Arthur. "The Copyright Bill: Grave Injustice in Proposals." The Times (London), 16 October 1956, p.11.

A letter to the Editor from ten composers, including Bliss, and four writers about the Copyright Bill, going through its parliamentary stages at that time.

B131.Bliss, Arthur. "Copyright Bill Proposal: music for social services bodies." The Times (London), 7 December 1955, p.11.

A letter from a number of composers, including Bliss, about the Copyright Bill which had recently been presented to Parliament.

B132.Bliss, Arthur. "Count C. Benckendorff." The Times (London), 6 October 1959, p.13.

A brief note about the Count, "obituary notices ... having not stressed his absorbing love of music, and, with his liberal and radical outlook, his passion for modern music."

B133.Bliss, Arthur. "Death on Squares." Great Thoughts, January 1938, pp.18-22.

An article with which Bliss "... tells the story of the ballet Checkmate and its composition." See: W5

B134.Bliss, Arthur. "Edward Elgar." The Musical Times 98 (June 1957), p.303.

A few lines, written for the Elgar centenary in 1957; "... at least eight of his major works will by their originality and mastery long outlive his age."

B135.Bliss, Arthur. "English music defended." The Daily Mail (London), 29 September 1921, p.4.

A defence of English music, prompted by pronouncements of Mr. Walter Damrosch, director of the New York Symphony Orchestra, and published in

*Musical America*, that "... the English school is merely grovelling in ugliness."

B136. Bliss, Arthur. "First Pages: 1891-1901." *Performing Right*, no.47 (April 1967), pp.2-5.

The first section of Bliss's autobiography (*As I Remember*), published under separate cover.

B137.    Bliss, Arthur. "Gerald Finzi." *The Times* (London), 3 October 1956, p.13.

Some lines written on the death of Gerald Finzi. "The death of this highly gifted composer is a severe loss to English music and a deep sorrow to his many friends. He was a lover of English poetry, and had a wide knowledge of it ...."

B138. Bliss, Arthur. "A German Festival." *Pall Mall Gazette* (London), 11 October 1916, p.8.

A letter from Capt. Arthur Bliss expressing his thanks to Edwin Evans and "Musicus" for their championship of English music and their fight against the predominating influence of Germany at home."

B139. Bliss, Arthur. "The Gramophone Jubilee Book." London. General Gramophone Publications. 1973.

A forward to the publication issued to celebrate *The Gramophone's* fifty years. "As it reaches its Golden Jubilee, I salute the fine service it has done for music."

B140. Bliss, Arthur. "Great music should be seen as well as heard." *TV Times* (London), 31 January 1964, p.6.

An article in which Bliss maintains that fine music and television do not go together after enough, and offers some ideas of how they could.

B141. Bliss, Arthur. "Handel's Operas." *The Times* (London), 15 May 1959, p.13.

A letter form leading musicians, Bliss amongst them, about the Handel bicentenary and an appeal for the staging of some of his operas.

B142. Bliss, Arthur. "Harold Brooke." *The Musical Times* 97 (November 1956), p.578.

An appreciation of Harold Brooke, a close friend of Arthur Bliss's, his publisher and a good practical musician.

B143. Bliss, Arthur, "Henry Purcell (1658-1695)." *The Chesterian* (London), no.17 (September 1921),pp.13-15.

An account about Henry Purcell, one of Arthur Bliss's favourite composers, with the suggestion that "... it is only just and right that the masterpieces ... should be welcomed with an every increasing admiration."

B144. Bliss, Arthur. "Impressions and Thanks." The British Bandsman, 3 October 1936, p.3.

Bliss's impressions of the National Band Festival held at the Crystal Palace, London in 1936 when Kenilworth was used as the test piece. The composer also seems to have been fully satisfied with its first performance. "There are very few times in a composer's life when the actual performance comes up to the ideal dreamed of, but I can truthfully say that last Saturday was one such occasion. The mastery of technique and the musical understanding were alike superb." See: W165a

B145. Bliss, Arthur. "Inventory of musical sources." The Times (London), 15 August 1963, p.9.

A letter, signed by Jack Westrup, C.B. Oldman and Arthur Bliss about the International Inventory of Musical Sources, "... which will comprehend all music existing in manuscript or print, written or published before 1801."

B146. Bliss, Arthur. "Is Music useless?" The Sunday Times (London), 19 October 1952, p.9.

A discussion about music in answer to "... Dr. Vaughan Williams (who) gave us one of his periodic apophthegms and told us that the honour and glory of our great art is that it is absolutely and entirely useless."

B147. Bliss, Arthur. "The Lady of Shalott." Artefact (Loughborough), 3 (May 1975), pp.4-5.

An article describing the composer's ballet The Lady of Shalott and its Leicestershire premiere. See: W7b

B148. Bliss, Arthur. "Let us take the initiative." Composer, no.14. (Autumn 1964), p.3.

As President of the Performing Right Society, Bliss makes the dynamic suggestion that the PRS should stage its own concerts, especially of English music.

B149. Bliss, Arthur. "London leads in Music." The Daily Mail (London), 20 October 1921, p.6.

A brief note claiming that London had now overtaken Vienna, Paris and other European cities as leader of the world's music.

B150.Bliss, Arthur. "A Lady Figure in Music." The Radio
     Times (London), (43) 15 June 1934, p.819.

     A tribute to Gustav Holst whose "... untimely death
     ... removes an outstanding figure to whom English
     music owes a greater debt than can be alluded to in
     these few words."

B151.Bliss, Arthur. "Malipiero : lover of animals." The
     Daily Telegraph (London), 28 January 1928, p.7.

     A thumb-nail sketch of Malipiero's work, music and
     personality, prompted by a performance of one of
     his works.

B152.Bliss, Arthur. "Michael Tippett." Contribution to a
     symposium on his 60th birthday, edited by Ian Kemp.
     London. Faber and Faber, 1965, p.34.

     A tribute to Tippett, "... that rare being among
     composers, or so it seems to me, whose heart and
     head are in happy conjunction. I am continually
     moved by the fervour in his music and at the same
     time kept aware of the keen intelligence that
     controls it."

B153.Bliss, Arthur. "More music from the BBC." The Times
     (London), 4 December 1958, p.13.

     A letter, signed amongst other by Bliss, about the
     retrograde policy of the BBC in cutting its output
     of sound broadcasting, and the resulting effects.

B154.Bliss, Arthur. "Music and Imagination by Aaron
     Copland." The Musical Times 95 January 1954,
     pp.21-22.

     A review of six lectures, printed in book form,
     given at Harvard University during the academic
     year 1951-2.

B155.Bliss, Arthur. "Music and the Films." Musical News and
     Herald, 18 February 1922, p.220.

     An article about providing suitable original music
     for "those damned films!"

B156.Bliss, Arthur. "Music in America : An impression". The
     Sackbut (London), September 1925, pp.30-1.

     Written on his return from America, Bliss states
     that "... in America lies the future of music. On
     the West side of the Atlantic are found more and
     finer orchestras, larger audiences, countless more
     clubs for the study of music, infinitely more
     schools, and withal every sign of still further
     development. Hardly a year passes without its crop
     of new orchestras and musical institutions, into
     which European artists are being continually

absorbed - a process which in time will inflict the
Old World with pernicious anaemia."

B157.Bliss, Arthur. "Musical Then and Now." Music Journal,
December 1966, pp.17 and 46.

A comparison, of what life used to be for
musicians, composers, orchestras, between now and
"the old days ... when the musicians was regarded
as a sort of vagabond...."

B158.Bliss, Arthur. "A Musical Embassy to the U.S.S.R." The
Times (London), 1 June 1956, pp.11-12.

A very detailed account of the three week concert
tour in the U.S.S.R., undertaken by eight English
musicians, and Trudy Bliss.

B159.Bliss, Arthur. "A Musical Pilgrimage of Britain: I -
Westwards, Bath and Bristol." The Listener XIV, 2
October 1935, pp.585-6.

The first article, in a series, in which Bliss set
out with the object of discovering the state of
musical life in the country, and finding if
possible what changes were taking place, and what
effect the BBC and broadcasting might have had on
these changes. This deals with music making in
Bath and Bristol.

B160.Bliss, Arthur. "A Musical Pilgrimage of Britain: II -
Cardiff and the Three Valleys." The Listener, XIV, 9
October 1935, pp.633-4.

An account of Bliss's visit to musical Cardiff and
South Wales where "singing is in their blood."

B161.Bliss, Arthur. "A Musical Pilgrimage of Britain: III -
Shropshire." The Listener, XIV, 16 October 1935,
pp.683-4.

A description of Bliss's journey "... from Cardiff
to Newport then up the valley of the Usk and Wye,
through the cathedral town of Hereford to that
lovliest of counties, Shropshire."

B162.Bliss, Arthur. "A Musical Pilgrimage of Britain: IV -
Music in the Five Towns." The Listener, XIV, 23
October 1935, pp.731-2.

"This district of the Potteries contains one of the
most famous choruses in England. The North
Staffordshire District Choral Society has made a
considerable amount of musical history since its
birth in 1901." Bliss goes on to the describe his
impressions of rehearsals.

B163.Bliss, Arthur. "A Musical Pilgrimage of Britain: V -
Four Lancashire Towns." The Listener, XIV, 30
October 1935, pp.779-780.

Bliss's impressions of visits to Rochdale,
birthplace of Gracie Fields and Norman Allin,
Burnley, Blackburn and Bolton.

B164.Bliss, Arthur. "A Musical Pilgrimage of Britain: VI -
Some West Riding Choruses." The Listener, XIV, 6
November 1935, pp.835-6.

Journeys to Leeds and Huddersfield which "... is
exceptional in its appreciation of music." A final
paragraph deals with Durham Cathedral.

B165.Bliss, Arthur. "A Musical Pilgrimage of Britain: VII -
Newcastle." The Listener, XIV, 13 November 1935,
pp.891-2.

A visit to the North East, with a description of
some of the variety and societies which "... is
bewildering."

B166.Bliss, Arthur, "A Musical Pilgrimage of Britain: VIII -
Glasgow." The Listener, XIV, 20 November 1935,
pp.939-940.

A continuation north to Glasgow which "... holds
for anyone who wants to explore, artistic treasures
of priceless value."

B167.Bliss, Arthur. "A Musical Pilgrimage of Britain: IX -
Southwards." The Listener, XIV, 27 November 1935,
pp.987-8.

Reports of visits to Lincoln and Peterborough.

B168.Bliss, Arthur. "A Musical Pilgrimage of Britain: X -
Cornwall." The Listener, XIV, 4 December 1935,
pp.1035-6.

Impressions of journeys to Liskeard, Wadebridge and
Penzance.

B169.Bliss, Arthur. "A Musical Pilgrimage of Britain: XI -
Ipswich and Norwich." The Listener, XIV, 11 December
1935, pp.1083-4.

An account of musical life in Ipswich and Norwich,
with a mention of the forthcoming new choral work
by Ralph Vaughan Williams for the Norwich Triennial
Festival.

B170.Bliss, Arthur. "A Musical Pilgrimage of Britain: XII -
Conclusion." The Listener, XIV, 18 December 1935,
pp.133-4.

Bliss concludes that although he has travelled
2,500 miles and seen many activities in various
branches in music, there are "... vast tracks of
musical enterprise not yet seen." He continues by
mentioning the world of brass bands, organs and
organ playing, professional orchestras - "...

indeed the quantity of music everywhere ... has most astonished me." The effect of broadcasting on music making is discussed, with his suggestions for the future.

B171.Bliss, Arthur.    "National Music Council Conference in Guildhall."  Living Music, Spring 1959, p.4.

A letter from Bliss to the Chairman of the National Music Council of Great Britain about putting the UK's symphony orchestras on a lasting basis of financial security, and a plea for the abolition of taxes on music as they fall most heavily on the young.

B172.Bliss, Arthur. "A New Work on Orchestration."  Musical News and Herald, 19 March 1921, p.363.

A review of Florence G. Fidler's Handbook of Orchestration.  "... I have searched in vain to find any suggestion that it is valuable for the understanding of contemporary scores."

B173.Bliss, Arthur.  "No cuts on music."  The Times (London), 2 July 1969, p.2.

An announcement that, as a result of talks with the BBC, the amount of serious music broadcast on Radio 3 "will be exactly the same as at present, but they were hoping that there would be more recorded music than live music."

B174.Bliss, Arthur.  "Noel Mewton Wood."  The Times (London), 8 December 1953, p.10.

An obituary of the famous pianist whose death  "... deprives us of a most loveable and gifted personality."

B175.Bliss, Arthur.  "Opinions."  The Chesterian, No.68, January/February 1928, pp.109-110.

Bliss's views "... about so elusive a subject as Inspiration .... Like electricity one is well aware of its presence, though hazy as to its source."

B176.Bliss, Arthur.  "Orchestra plan for disused church." The Times (London), 8 April 1972, p.13.

A letter supporting the idea that one of London's fine old churches, Holy Trinity, Southwark, should be used by the LSO and the LPO, acting jointly after restoration as their permanent recording and rehearsal hall.

B177.Bliss, Arthur. "Orchestral Wind Instruments, Ancient and Modern."  Musical News and Herald, 9 April 1921, p.465.

Review of "a very valuable book ... so eminently readable that a large circle of musicians generally will be glad to make its acquaintance."

B178.Bliss, Arthur. "Visit to Russia." News: A Soviet Review of World Events (Moscow), no.10, 10 May 1956, p.19.

Arthur Bliss's views on music in light of his visit to Russia. "It helps a nation to get a better understanding of the character, thoughts and feelings of another."

B179.Bliss, Arthur. "A Personal Reminiscence of Shosta- kovitch." World of Music, no.6, March 1962, p.6.

A brief sketch of Shostakovitch, based on Bliss's meetings with him in Russia and London.

B180.Bliss, Arthur. "The President's Speech." Performing Right October 1966, p.4.

The text of Bliss's speech, as President of the PRS, to the 1966 Annual Luncheon, and his welcome to the chief Guest of Honour, Sir Alan Herbert.

B181.Bliss, Arthur. "Professor E.J. Dent." The Times (London), 11 November 1958, p.11.

A letter appealing for donations to the Royal Musical Association's fund "... of which the primary purpose would be the annual award of a medal for outstanding services to musicology..." in memory of Professor Edward J. Dent.

B182.Bliss, Arthur. "Ralph Vaughan Williams." The Musical Times, 99 (October 1958), pp.537-8.

A tribute to Vaughan Williams who "... has been the great name in our music for many years."

B183.Bliss, Arthur. "Recent works of Arnold Bax." Musical News and Herald, 21 May 1921, p.652.

Reviews of newly published scores by Bax, including chamber works, songs and solo piano pieces.

B184.Bliss, Arthur. "Recent works of Igor Stravinsky." Musical News and Herald, 14 May 1921, p.625.

Review of newly-published scores by Stravinsky including Pulcinella and the suite from L'Histoire du Soldat.

B185.Bliss, Arthur. "Record Royalities." The Times (London), 2 July 1956, p.9.

A letter to The Times about "... the inadequacy of the mechanical royalty of 6.25% payable in respect of words and music under the terms of the new Copyright Bill."

B186.Bliss, Arthur.   "Reflections on Three Works of Eugene
       Goossens."   <u>Musical News and Herald</u>, 4 June 1921,
       p.721.

       A detailed account of three compositions, with
       recollections of their first performances.

B187.Bliss, Arthur.   "Remarkable Players and a Critical
       Audience."  <u>Moscow News</u>, 16 April 1958, p.2.

       An account of the proceedings of the Tchaikovsky
       Competition for Pianists, for which event Bliss was
       one of the judges.

B188.Bliss, Arthur. "Reviews of new music." <u>Musical News and
       Herald</u>, 25 June 1921, p. 817.

       Descriptions of three works for piano by William
       Baines and three sets of songs by Lord Berners.

B189.Bliss, Arthur. "Royal Philharmonic Society." <u>The Times</u>
       (London), 27 August 1962, p.9.

       A letter about the forthcoming 150th anniversary of
       the RPS, early in 1963.

B190.Bliss, Arthur.  "The Royal Philharmonic Society."
       London, RPS, 1962, pp.11 and 13.

       A forward to the 150th birthday programme book in
       which Bliss traces its history, and looks ahead to
       the future.

B191.Bliss, Arthur.   "The Shanty Book."  <u>Queen</u>, 12 November
       1921, p.628.

       A review of a book of shanties, collected and
       edited by Richard Runciman Terry who, writes Bliss,
       should "... receive the welcome thanks of all jaded
       musicians."

B192.Bliss, Arthur.  "Shape of musical things to come."
       <u>Leicester Evening Mail</u>, 10 October 1958, p.16.

       An article in which Bliss talks about his version
       of John Gay's opera <u>The Beggar's Opera</u>, and the
       concert version, first performance in Leicester.
       <u>See</u>: W132b

B193.Bliss, Arthur, "Sheila Mossman." <u>The Times</u> (London), 21
       August 1971, p.12.

       An appreciation of the life of Sheila Mossman,
       "... an inspired teacher of young singers."

B194.Bliss, Arthur.   "A Short Note on Stravinsky's
       Orchestration."  <u>The Musical Standard</u>, 30 July 1921,
       p.43.

A discussion about Stravinsky's "... orchestration as opposed to instrumentation." Several works of Stravinsky are cited as examples.

B195.Bliss, Arthur. "Some answers to some questions." Music, December 1951, pp.17-19.

A very enlightening interview and discussion about composing, influences and problems facing composers.

B196.Bliss, Arthur. "Some aspects of the present musical situation." Proceedings of the Royal Musical Association, 49, 13 March 1923, pp.59-77.

Details of a paper given to the RMA by Arthur Bliss, together with the discussion that followed.

B197.Bliss, Arthur. "Special duty of the BBC." The Times (London), 26 April 1957, p.11.

A letter concerning "... our deep concern at the new trend of policy in sound broadcasting recently announced by the BBC."

B198.Bliss, Arthur. "Starved to death." The Times (London), 23 October 1972, p.13.

The composer's concern about a two-year-old baby strapped in his pram and left by his mother to starve to death.

B199.Bliss, Arthur. "The Story of Checkmate." Record Review, 4 (June 1960), p.5.

A short description of Checkmate, the first of Bliss's four ballets, and the best known. See: W5

B200.Bliss, Arthur. "Stray Musings in Amsterdam." Royal College of Music Magazine, 16 (1920), pp.17-20.

An account of the musical life of Holland, and the composer's impressions.

B201.Bliss, Arthur. " A Symphony of Composers." Occasion, no6. (1964), pp.10-11.

A review and discussion about the work of the Composers' Guild of Great Britain, whose president Arthur Bliss was for many years.

B202.Bliss, Arthur. "Tribute to Stravinsky." The Times (London), 7 April 1971, p.1.

A brief appreciation about "... one of those geniuses who come only, once or twice in a century."

B203.Bliss, Arthur. "Verdi: a symposium." Opera, 11, February 1951, pp.112-3.

Bliss's views about the music of Verdi, especially his operas.

B204. Bliss, Arthur. "Welcome to Schoenberg!" Musical News, no. 1824, January 1928, p.12.

A discussion about Schoenberg, his work and music, prompted by a forthcoming visit to the composer to conduct his Gurrelieder.

B205. Bliss, Arthur. "What Broadcasting has done for music." The Listener, VIII, 16 November 1932, pp.704-5.

A survey of the first ten years of music-making by the BBC, with particular mention of the BBC Symphony Orchestra.

B206. Bliss, Arthur. "What modern composition is aiming at." Musical News and Herald 23 July 1921, p.90; 6 August 1921, pp.138-9; 20 August 1921, pp.189-190.

The text of Bliss's paper read at the Society of Women Musicians on 2 July 1921.

B207. Blom, Eric. "The Clarinet Quintet of Arthur Bliss." The Musical Times, 74 (May 1935), pp.424-7.

A detailed analysis, movement by movement, with musical examples. See: W55

B208. Blom, Eric. "A Garland for the Queen." The Observer (London), 7 June 1953, p.11f.

A review of the first performance which included Bliss's setting, Aubade for a Coronation Morning. See: W74a

B209. Blom, Eric. "Morning Heroes." The Music Teacher, March 1931, pp.149-150.

A brief description of Bliss's choral symphony, written as an introduction for the work's first London performance in March 1931. See: B84b

B210. Blom, Eric. "Studies at Random: VI - An Ideal Concerto." Musical Opinion, August 1921, pp.928-9.

As essay about the concerto, with particular reference to Bliss's Concerto for piano and tenor voice. See:W12

B211. Blom, Eric. "Towards Perfect Bliss." Musical News and Herald, 18 September 1926, pp.226-7.

A survey of Bliss's career up to the Introduction and Allegro, a work with which "... he has matured out of all knowledge." See: B20a

B212. Bonavia, F. "London hears new music." The New York Times 24 November 1935, Section IX, p.6.

An account of some recent performances in London, including that of Bliss's Music for Strings.  "Its outstanding qualities are a rich sonority and the very happy, cheerful mood, which breaks out in the first, also completely dominated the last section."

B213.Boult, Adrian. "Sir Arthur Bliss." Royal College of Music Magazine, LXVII (Summer Term 1971), p.61.

A tribute to Arthur Bliss on his 80th birthday which he celebrated on 2 August 1971. He recalls their first meeting and says "... his quickness of wit makes him excellent company, and he has cleverly told many other stories in his recent autobiography, a memorable book."

B214.Badbury, Ernest. "Sir Arthur Bliss." Yorkshire Post (Leeds), 29 March 1975, p.3.

An obituary recalling Sir Arthur as "... a young composer who was described as as ruffian, a hothead and semi-wild who grew into a pillar of the musical establishment whose works graced the greatest State occasions."

B215.Bradbury, Ernest. "Mary of Magdala." The Musical Times, 104 (October 1963), p.722.

A review of the cantata's first performance in Worcester Cathedral, as part of the 3-Choirs Festival. See: W83a

B216.Brook, David.   "Arthur Bliss - in his Composers' Gallery: Biographical Sketches of Contemporary Composers." London, Rockcliff, 1946, pp.23-8.

A brief biographical sketch of the composer, with mention of the major works.

B217.Burn, Andrew. "Now, Trumpeter for thy Close." The Musical Times, 126 (November 1985), pp.666-668.

A detailed background account of Bliss's choral symphony Morning Heroes, with musical examples. See: W84

B218."Cadwall." "An explorer of sound." The Musical Mirror, (September 1921), pp.7-8.

An informal interview with Arthur Bliss, "... the most daring of our young musicians. At twenty-eight he has made an indelible mark on the lustre of music in England. Like himself his music pulsated with vitality."

B219.Capell, Richard. "Blare Music." The Daily Mail (London), 21 April 1921, p.5.

A review of the concert, given at the Aeolian Hall, London by Edward Clark and his orchestra which included <u>Conversations</u>. "Mr. Bliss ... writes the best music...." <u>See</u>: W37a

B220.Cardus, Neville; Rosenthall, Harold; Noteutt,A. and Buckle, Richard. "The Olympians." <u>Opera</u>, 1 (February 1950), pp.10-15.

A discussion about Bliss's opera <u>The Olympians</u>, and the state of English opera.

B221.Cardus, Neville. "The Venerable Square." <u>The Guardian</u> (Manchester), 2 August 1961, p.7.

A salute to Arthur Bliss on his 70th birthday "... composer of one of the best English ballets, composer of film music ...."

B222.Chislett, W.A. "Fanfares." <u>Gramophone</u>, 55 (June 1977),pp67-8.

Review of the Locke Consort of Brass recording which included Bliss's <u>Fanfare for a Coming of Age</u>, <u>Fanfare for the Lord Mayor of London</u>, <u>Fanfare for a Dignified Occasion</u>, <u>Fanfare for Heroes</u>, <u>Fanfares for the weddings of Princess Alexandra and Margaret</u> and <u>Salute to Shakespeare</u>. "Here is a brilliant conception superbly carried out." <u>See</u>: D6,D21, D22,D23,D41,D43,D58

B223.Chissell, Joan. "Bliss Birthday Concert." <u>The Times</u> (London), 3 August 1971, p.7.

An account of the Bliss - 80th birthday Promenade Concert, held in the Royal Albert Hall. "The interval ... brought a personal thank-you from Sir Arthur after Lennox Berkeley, on behalf of the musical profession at large, presented him with a record of his works, several new to the gramophone."

B224.Chissell, Joan. "Croydon Arts Festival." <u>The Times</u> (London), 23 April 1973, p.5.

"... and before... Vernon Handley ... introduced a work commissioned by the festival from ... Sir Arthur Bliss. Entitled <u>Variations for Orchestra</u> [Metamorphic Variations], this 40 minute piece is dedicated "in token of a long and cherished friendship" to George and Ann Dannatt. Not only do their initials make the subject of the sturdy interlude called "dedication" towards the end, but Bliss's choice of variation form was in fact sparked off by a group of abstract paintings by George Dannatt in the nature of variants of a theme. Bliss's thematic starting point is a group of motifs (or "elements"), in turn a long oboe cantilena, a brief chordal phrase for horns, and an ethereal note-cluster. After the joyous climax of the last variation called "affirmation" (each number has its own mood heading) the work ends with

a quiet restatement of opening ideas ... always the
composer seems to be drawing on a golden trove of
personal memory." <u>See</u>: W24a

B225.Chissell, Joan. "Louis Kentner: Queen Elizabeth Hall."
<u>The Times</u> (London), 22 March 1971, p.8.

"The special interest of Louis Kentner's piano
recital yesterday afternoon was the first
performance of a <u>Triptych</u> dedicated to him by Sir
Arthur Bliss, "in admiration and gratitude." In
his programme note Sir Arthur reminded us that the
piano was his first love. Each of the three new
pieces suggested undiminished appreciation of the
instrument's potential." <u>See</u>: W68a

B226.Chissell, Joan.  "A ride with Dr. Who."  <u>The Times</u>
(London), 17 July 1972, p.7.

"At last night's closing concert in the Town Hall,
his first quartet was followed by his second, or
rather its slow movement and Scherzo - specially
adapted by the composer as <u>Two Contrasts for String
Orchestra</u>.... Without noticeable changes of text
or texture, they make a excellent, self-contained
pair, gaining intensity from reinforcement in the
more impassioned middle section of the sostenuto,
and heightened colour in the contrasting episodes
of the Scherzo." <u>See</u>: W54b

B227.Cole, Hugo. "The Energy of Bliss." <u>Country Life</u>, 29
July 1976, p.290.

An account of some of the retrospective concerts of
Bliss's music, given early in July 1976 at the
Cheltenham Festival, which "... confirm impressions
of Bliss as a consistent and tireless craftsman
whose work radiated optimism and energy."

B228.Cole, Hugo. "Memory of war inspired his music." <u>The
Guardian</u> (Manchester), 29 March 1975, p.6.

An obituary of Bliss, mentioning that "memories of
the war remained with him for life, as did a
military ... manner, though warmth, kindness and
humour were never far below the surface."

B229.Cooper, Martin.  "Arthur Bliss - <u>in his</u> Les Musiciens
anglais d'aujourd'hui." Paris, Librarie Plon, 1952,
pp.77-91.

A biographical sketch, with mention in the book of
Bliss's major works, written in French.

B230.Cooper, Martin. "Hidden Sensibility." <u>The Daily
Telegraph</u> (London), 29 March 1975, p.10.

An appreciation of Bliss's life in which he is
described as "... a lively-minded man of many
interests, in whom wit and charm disguised a

sensibility that he instinctively hid.  He was a
shrewd judge of his own gifts, as he showed in his
autobiography, an astonishingly truthful and vivid
picture of the author both as man and artist."

B231.Cooper, Martin.  "A Queen's man of the arts."  The Daily
    Telegraph (London), 9 May 1970, p.10.

    An extended review of Bliss's autobiography As I
    Remember.

B232.Cox, David.  "A view of Bliss's music."  The Listener,
    LXXIV 18 November 1965, p.813.

    A discussion about the achievement of Sir Arthur
    Bliss, with particular reference to the Colour
    Symphony and Music for Strings.

B233.Craggs, S.R. "Sir Arthur Bliss : A Preliminary Survey
    and Synthesis of Materials for the Study of his
    Music."  Dissertation  -  Ph.D.,  University  of
    Strathclyde, Glasgow, Scotland. 1982. 4 Volumes.

    The first volume deals with Bliss's life and the
    critical reactions to his music.  Volumes 2,3 and 4
    form  a  complete  thematic  catalogue  of  Bliss's
    musical works, published and unpublished, arranged
    chronologically  by  date  of  composition,  with
    musical examples.  The present volume is based on
    this thesis.

B234.Crichton,  Ronald.  "Bliss  and  his  music  kept  their
    zest."  The Financial Times (London), 29 March 1975,
    p.6.

    An obituary in which Bliss is described as "... a
    classic example of the avant-garde artist gradually
    changing into an Establishment figure, the young
    musical radical of the 20's ending as a respected
    senior composer with a solid list of works in
    accepted geneus to his credit."

B235.Crichton,  Ronald.  "Bliss's  Triptych."  The  Musical
    Times, 112 (May 1971), p.463.

    "In his 80th year, he has rekindled the old flame
    with three short pieces called Triptych, dedicated
    to Louis Kentner...."  See: W68a

B236.Crichton, Ronald.  "Croydon Arts Festival."  The Musical
    Times, 114 (June 1973), pp.624-5.

    A review of Bliss's Metamorphic Variations which
    "... is more solid and more considered than the
    common run of festival commissions...."  See: W24a

B237.Crisp, Clement. "The Ballets of Arthur Bliss."  The
    Musical Times, 107 (August 1966), pp. 674-5.

A description and discussion Sir Arthur Bliss and his four ballet scores.

B238. Dale, S.S.  "Contemporary Cello Concerti - VII: Sir Arthur Bliss."  The Strand, 83 (April 1973), pp.629-635.

An analysis of the Cello Concerto, together with a brief history of Bliss's career and mention of some other major works.  See: W14

B239. Demuth, Norman.  "Arthur Bliss."  The Sackbut, September 1930, pp.46-9.

An account and description of the "... three Arthur Blisses : one who before the war composed (presumably) music that was discarded, another who at the end of the war rose high on the war of fashion and vanished at its breaking, and a third who has recently put aside childish things and turned to serious."

B240. Downes, Olin.  "Checkmate Suite has premiere here."  The New York Times, 17 November 1939, p.18.

A review of the first performance in America of the suite for Checkmate.  "The music is admirably orchestrated, and it is real ballet music.  It has the quality of the scene, the theatre.  The rhythms and figures of various dances are clear, yet there is a considerable measure of symphonic development ...."  See: W5d

B241. Downs, Olin.  "Colour Symphony Played."  The New York Times, 6 January 1924, Section 1 Part 2, p.6.

An account of the Colour Symphony's first perfor- mance in New York.  "Mr. Bliss writes brilliantly ... sometimes he achieves passages of exceptional beauty ... and more than once he evolves a passage of counterpoint or harmonic dissonance which makes one wish to stop the orchestra and hear that over again."  See: W10c

B242. Downes, Olin.  "Two new works directed by Boult."  The New York Times, 11 June 1939, p.47.

A review of the concert at the New York World Fair which included Bliss's Piano Concerto.  "The form is a big one and is well handled.  Mr Bliss is writing for a virtuoso and knows it; at the same time he is symphonic.  This a superior kind of a piece for an occasion, and a modern pianist's vehicle."  See: W11a

B243. Drew, David.  "The Decca Book of Ballet."  London, Muller, 1958, pp.79-83.

A detailed synopsis and analysis of Checkmate and Miracle in the Gorbals, dance by dance.  See: W5,W8

B244.Eggar, Katherine.  "The  Orchestral  Work  of  Arthur
      Bliss."  The Music Student, XIII (September 1921),
      pp.673-4.

      A survey of the work of Arthur Bliss, "... a very
      gifted and clear sighted young contemporary of our
      own.  His  orchestral  pieces  are  frankly  and
      definitely the expression of his interest in the
      sound aspect of music."

B245.Evans, Edwin. "Arthur Bliss."  The Musical Times, 64
      (January  1923),  pp.20-23;   64  (February  1923),
      pp.95-99.

      A very detailed account of Bliss's life and music,
      together with musical examples, a composer who was
      "... utterly unknown at the beginning of 1919, but
      was transformed into a celebrity before the end of
      1921."

B246.Evans, Edwin. "Perfect Bliss?"  The Listener, XXIII, 25
      January 1940, p. 193.

      A discussion of Bliss's compositions, noting that
      "his  advance  in  actual  musical  achievement  is
      enormous and incontestable."

B247.Evans, Edwin.  "The Tempest."  Musical News and Herald,
      5 February 1921, p.177.

      "Bliss  has  made  an  ingenious  and  dramatically
      effective use of percussion instruments, chiefly
      timpani, of which there are fifteen, requiring five
      players." See:W147a

B248.Felton, Felix.  "The Radio Play."  London, Sylvan Press,
      1949, pp.112-3.

      Mention of "... a piece of original writing for
      radio, Memorial Concert, by Trudy Bliss, the wife
      of Arthur Bliss, who composed the music specially
      for  the  programme.   For  anyone  exploring  the
      possibilities of such a theme, Memorial Concert was
      a  model  of  its  kind,  both  for  its  close
      inter-relation of music and dialogue, and for the
      way  in  which  the  literal  use  of  the  music  was
      combined  with  the  exploitation  of  its  power  to
      suggest emotional atmosphere." See: W144

B249.Ferrier, Winifred.   "The  Life  of  Kathleen  Ferrier."
      London, Hamilton 1955, p.160.

      A brief note about the circumstances surrounding
      the commissioning and subsequent first performance
      of The Enchantress by Kathleen Ferrier.  See: W78

B250.Fiske,  Roger.   "Aubade."   The  Gramophone,  65  (June
      1977), p.90.

A review of the re-recording (RCA - Gold Seal :GL 25062) of <u>A Garland for the Queen</u>, made in 1977, the Silver Jubilee Year of H.M. Queen Elizabeth II, which included Bliss's setting of Reed's poem, <u>Aubade</u>. <u>See</u>: D3

B251.Fiske, Roger. "Ballads of the Four Seasons: No.2." <u>The Gramophone</u>, 41 (November 1963) pp. 234-5.

Review of the Jupiter JEPOC-33 recording of English songs, sung by Dorothy Dorow. "Bliss beautifully catches the elusive mood of a Li Po poem...." <u>See</u>:D4

B252.Fiske, Roger. "Rich or Poor." <u>The Gramophone</u>, 44 (January 1967), pp.380-1.

Review of the HMV CSD 3587 recording of Twentieth Century English Songs, sung by Frederick Harvey. <u>See</u>: D53

B253.Fiske, Roger. "Sonata for Viola." <u>The Gramophone</u>, 42 (December 1964), p. 285.

Review of the Herbert Downes/Leonard Cassini recording (Delta DEL 12028) of Bax's and Bliss's viola sonatas. "The Bliss ... does not have quite as much immediate impact, but here too there is warm feeling and skilful writing." <u>See</u>: D62

B254.Foreman, Lewis. "Arthur Bliss: Catalogue of the complete Works." Borough Green, Novello, 1980, 159 pp.

This catalogue gives details of all Bliss's compositions, and also lists his published writings - to be of use to working musicians and researches. It also contains a discography, and is prefaced "... by an evocative and penetrating essay by George Dannatt, the composer's life-long friend and associate...."

B255.Foss, Hubert, J. "Arthur Bliss's Clarinet Quintet." <u>The Monthly Musical Record</u>, February 1933, pp.31-2.

An exposition of the <u>Clarinet Quintet</u>, movement by movement, with musical examples, "... a vital and delightful piece of music." <u>See</u>: W55

B256.Foss, Hubert. "Arthur Bliss's new ballet." <u>Tempo</u>, No.9, December 1944, p.14.

A brief review of <u>Miracle in the Gorbals</u>. "Certainly, one performance gave me a strong impression of the absoluteness of the music, of its completeness in conception and in realization. The other dominant feeling I had was of an enormous and passionate energy, wholehearted poured out and only with difficulty restrained and moulded into artistic shape." <u>See</u>:W8

B257.Foss, Hubert J. "Classicism and Arthur Bliss." The Musical Times, 75 March 1934, pp.213-17.

A very detailed analysis of the Viola Sonata, with musical examples. "... it occupies a place of importance in the career of Bliss as a composer, and unless I am greatly mistaken, a rare one in the annals of modern English music." See: W60

B258.Foss, Hubert. "The Olympians." The Canon, February 1950, pp.427-8.

Comments about Bliss's opera and its production at the Royal Opera House, Covent Garden. See: W2a

B259.Frank, Alan. "Bliss's new Violin Concerto." Radio Times, 6 May 1955, p.4.

An introduction to "... the event of the week... Sir Arthur Bliss's new Violin Concerto, commissioned by the BBC and specially written for that outstanding violinst, Campoli. This is his first concerto for any stringed instrument and I get the impression... that he has immensely enjoyed writing it and collaborating on the technical side with Campoli. In their frequent meetings over the last six months they have poured together over almost every bar." See: W13

B260.Frank, Alan. "Contemporary Portraits: no.7. - Sir Arthur Bliss." The Music Teacher and Piano Student, XXX October 1951, pp.447-8.

A general article on Bliss, his life and music in which he is described as "... as refreshingly human personality in English music."

(Reprinted and expanded in Alan Frank's "Modern British Composers". London, Dobson, 1953, pp.28-34.)

B261.Frankenstein, A. "The Lady of Shalott." The San Francisco Chronicle, 4 May 1958, p.30.

A review of the ballet, The Lady of Shalott, and its first performance by the San Francisco Ballet. See: W7a

B262.G.,J. "Arthur Bliss and a Discussion." Musical News and Herald, 24 March 1923, pp.288-90.

A paper given to the Musical Association about some aspects of the then present musical situation, followed by a record of the discussion.

B263."Gamba." "Violinists at Home and Abroad." The Strad, March 1921, pp.352-4.

A mention of the first performance of Two Studies for Orchestra at the Royal College of Music. "...

these were an inconsequent mixture of ... material and modernism but the effect was not half bad in its way." <u>See</u>: W30a

B264.Garden, Neville. "Composer who set the Gorbals to music". <u>Scottish Daily Express</u> (Edinburgh), 28 March 1975, p.2.

An obituary. describing Bliss as "... a man who put the Gorbals on the cultural map."

B265.Gipps, Ruth. "Arthur Bliss." <u>Composer</u>, no.20 (Summer 1966), pp.14-17.

An article concerned with Bliss's music and the various aspects of the emotions and moods expressed by it by a conductor who has directed many of his works with the Chanticleer Orchestra, and who dedicated her 5th symphony to Bliss.

B266.Gipps, Ruth. "Meditations on a Theme." <u>Composer</u>, no.41 (Autumn 1971), pp.9-15.

A personal view of the music of Arthur Bliss, dealing in particular with one work, <u>Meditations on a Theme by John Blow</u>. "Bliss's orchestration, craftsmanlike but comparatively orthodox in the early works, had achieved, by the date of the <u>Meditations</u>, a mastery almost unique among contemporary composers." Each meditation is examined in detail, illustrated by musical examples. <u>See</u>: W22

B267.Goddard, Scott. "Arthur Bliss's Colour Symphony." <u>Tempo</u>, March 1939, pp.5-6.

An article tracing the historial background of Bliss's <u>Colour Symphony</u>, and an account of the work, movement by movement. <u>See</u>: W10

B268.Goddard, Scott. "Bliss and the English Tradition." <u>The Listener</u>, XXXV, 28 March 1946, p.413.

A discussion about "... the English tradition being mainly choral..." and how Bliss's choral music, especially his <u>Pastoral</u> of 1929, fits into that tradition. "The music is some of the most accomplished ever created by Bliss."

B269.Goddard, Scott. "Bliss's Piano Concerto." <u>The Musical Times</u>, 103( November 1962), pp.761-2.

An article about the <u>Piano Concerto</u>, prompted by the "... appearance of a new recording... issued by HMV...." <u>See</u>: W11

B270.Goddard, Scott. "A Leading Figure in English Music." <u>The Radio Times</u>, 2 October 1936, p.13.

A general account of the composer's life and music, describing him as "... one of the brightest stars in the musical firmament just after the war.... He was one of these young men who led our generation and were always ahead of us rank and file."

B271.Goddard, Scott. "Muscular Music." News Chronicle (London), 25 April 1953, p.3.

A brief mention of the Piano Sonata's first performance. "The writing is energetic and muscular, the thought eloquent." See: W59a

B272.Goodwin, Felix. "The Consistent Mr. Bliss." The Sackbut, (London), December 1924, pp.139-140.

A comparison of English music with the English Turf, promted by the arresting headline "Mr. Bliss wins."

B273.Goodwin, N. "Knot of Riddles." The Musical Times, 104 (September 1963), pp.641-2.

A review of the 1963 Cheltenham Festival and mention of the first performance of Knot of Riddles, commissioned and broadcast by the BBC. See: W114a

B274.Goossens, Eugene. "Arthur Bliss." The Chesterian, no.16, June 1921, pp.481-6.

A survey of the composer's career, up to that date, and concluding that"... if Arthur Bliss will continue on the path he has started to tread, it is safe to prophesy for him a career which will contribute one more landmark in the history of English musical achievement."

B275.Grace, Harvey. "Morning Heroes." The Musical Times, 71 (October 1930), pp.881-6.

A very detailed account and analysis of Bliss's Morning Heroes, movement by movement, written to compliment the first performance at Norwich in October 1930. See: W84a

B276.Grant, Elspeth. "Light on Africa." Daily Graphic (London), 19 July 1946, p.2.

A review of the film, Men of Two Worlds, "... an usual and important film about East Africa.... the picture is impressive." See: W136a

B277.Greenfield, E. "Aldeburgh." The Musical Times, 111 (August 1970), pp.819-820.

An account of the Cello Concerto's first performance at the Aldeburgh Festival. "... the ideas are striking and the argument well-sustained.

It is one of his livliest works since the war."
See: W14a

B278. Greenfield, E.  "Concerto for 2 pianos (3 hands)."  The
Gramophone, 48 (October 1970), p.581

A review of the recording HMV ASD 2612 which
included the Bliss Concerto for two pianos.  See:
D15

B279. Greenfield, E.  "Conductor at work."  Record Review, 4
(April 1960), p.5.

An account of the recording session when Bliss
conducted some of his own works for the World
Record Club disc ST52.  See: D11

B280. Greenfield, E.  "Meditations on a theme by John Blow."
The Gramophone, 44 (October 1966), p.205.

A review of the Lyrita recording (SRCS 33) of the
Meditations and Music for Strings.  See: D34, D40

B281. Greenfield, E.  "Meditations on a theme by John Blow."
The Gramophone 58 (August 1980), pp.214-5.

A review of the HMV disc (ASD 3878) of the
Meditations, Discourse for Orchestra and Edinburgh,
the latter items "... important new additions" to
the catalogue.  See: D19,D20,D34

B282. Greenfield, E.  "Piano Concerto, etc."  The Gramophone,
59 (September 1981), p. 378.

A review of the Unicorn-Kanchana record (DKP 9006)
of Bliss's Piano Concerto, March of Homage and
Welcome the Queen, played the Royal Liverpool
Philharmonic Orchestra, conducted by David
Atherton, with Philip Fowke as soloist.  See:
D14,D33,D66

B283. Greenfield, E.  "Piano solo pieces."  The Gramophone, 54
(August 1976), p.320.

A review of Richard Rodney Bennett playing some
twentieth-century British piano music on Polydor
Super 2383-391 including Bliss: One-Step and the
Rout Trot which "... brings the most brilliant of
all Bennett's performances."  See: D8, D55

B284. Gregson, Edward.  "The Brass Music of Sir Arthur Bliss."
Sounding Brass and the Conductor, 1 (January 1973),
pp.118-9.

A general article about Bliss's music for brass
band including mention of Kenilworth and the
Belmont Variations, together with some of his
fanfares.  See: W149, W165.

B285.Griffiths, P. and Badder, D.J. "Sir Arthur Bliss." Film Dope, no.5. (July 1974), pp.2-5.

> An interview with the composer about all his major film scores. See: W132,W134,W135,W136,W138,W139, W140

B286.Guilbert, F. "Arthur Bliss's Clarinet Quintet." The Gramophone, 16 (August 1938), p.140.

> A general introduction to and analysis of the Clarinet Quintet.

B287.Guyett, Andrew. "A Bliss Discography." Journal of the British Music Society, 2 (1980), pp.28-37.

> A detailed discography, arranged by title and giving full details of available recordings, both 78rpm and 33rpm.

B288.Guyett, Andrew. "A Discography of Bliss." Le Grand Baton: Journal of the Sir Thomas Beecham Society, 14 (March 1977), pp.11-22.

> A very useful list of recordings, issued up to 1976.

B289.Guyett, Andrew. "Sir Arthur Bliss (1891-1975): Master of the Queen's Musick." Le Grand Baton, 14 (March 1977), p.3-8.

> An appreciation of Bliss's life and music.

B290.Hale, P. "Two 2-Piano Pieces Played first time." The Boston Herald, 20 December 1924, p.28.

> Review of the first performance of Bliss's Concerto for 2 pianos and Orchestra. "Mr. Bliss is not a man to be flippantly dismissed as a freak. He has been consistent in the carrying out of his musical convictions. He has ideas: he has unusual ways of expressing them." See: W12b

B291.Harvey, T. "Adam Zero." The Gramophone, 49 (September 1971), p.457.

> A review of the Lyrita (SRCS 47) recording which included three dances from Adam Zero. See: D1

B292.Harvey, T. "Concerto for piano and orchestra." The Gramophone, 40 (December 1962), p.288.

> A review of the stereophonic version of the HMV recording of the Piano Concerto (ASD 499). "Bliss's invention and his infallible craftsmanship are at their best; the work is full of immensely arresting ideas and they are developed with a combination of imagination and technical skill." See: D14

B293.Harvey, T.  "Melee Fantasque."  The Gramophone, 49 (June 1971), pp.42 and 45.

A review of the Lyrita (SRCS 50) recording of British music which included Melee Fantasque, conducted by the composer. See: D35

B294.Harvey, T.  "Orchestral Works."  The Gramophone, 32 (January 1955), pp.344-5.

A review of the Columbia recording (33CX 1205) featuring the suite for Miracle in the Gorbals and Music for Strings, both conducted by the composer. See: D37, D40

B295.Harvey, T.  "Orchestral Works."  The Gramophone, 36 (April 1959), p.513.

A review of the RCA Victor (SB 2026) recording of the suite from Things to Come and Bliss's march Welcome the Queen. See: D63, D66

B296.Harvey, T.  "Welcome the Queen."  The Gramophone, 32 (July 1954), p.57.

A review of the Columbia (DX 1912) recording of Welcome the Queen. See: D66

B297.Haskell, Arnold.  "Miracle in the Gorbals: a Study." Edinburgh,  The Albyn Press, 1946.

A study of Bliss's ballet Miracle in the Gorbals, including a section on the music. See: W8

B298.Hassall, C. "Tobias and the Angel."  Radio Times, 13 May 1960, p.3.

The librettist of Bliss's opera Tobias and the Angel looks forward to the first performance and provides listeners with an introduction to the plot. See: W3

B299.Heath, Edward.  "Music: A Joy for Life."  London, Sidgwick and Jackson, 1976, p.143.

A description of the events when Mar Portugues was performed in the Painted Hall at Greenwich.  "It is a splendid piece, to my mind amongst the most effective of Arthur Bliss's smaller choral works." The dinner at Downing Street, in honour of the 70th birthday of Sir William Walton, is also recalled. "... Arthur Bliss wrote a witty piece to some amusing words by the poet Paul Dehn... entitled An Ode for William Walton." See: W82a,W87a

B300.Henry, L. "Contemporaries : Arthur Bliss."  Musical Opinion,  October 1922,  p.47-48;  December 1922, p.250-1; January 1923, p.351-2.

A very detailed article about Bliss and his music, up to the <u>Colour Symphony</u>.

B301.Henry, L. "Recent Recitals." <u>The Musical Standard</u>, 23 October 1920, p.146.

A review of the first performance of <u>Rhapsody</u>. "Bliss has as yet produced little, but every work bears marks of an unique personality. His <u>Rhapsody</u> is one of the few works precisely corresponding to that title, exquisitely coloured, but without preciousness or anaemic poeticism." <u>See</u>: W116a

B302.Henry, L. "Salutations - II : Arthur Bliss." <u>The Musical Standard</u>, 15 January 1921, pp.26-7.

A tribute to Bliss "... amongst the most intelligent and imaginative of our younger creative musical minds...."

B303.Hopkins, A. "The Ballet Music of Arthur Bliss." in <u>The Ballet Annual</u>. London, A & C Black, 1947, pp.102-4 and 107.

An account of Bliss's ballet scores, including the latest <u>Adam Zero</u> in which "... Arthur Bliss has shown that he is a true craftsman of the theatre, realising fully the difficulties of the union of music and ballet...." <u>See</u>: W4,W5,W8

B304.Howells, H. "Master of the Queen's Music." <u>Royal College of Music Magazine</u>, January 1954, pp.6-7.

An appreciation of Bliss's life and music on his appointment as Master of the Queen's Music which "... has given immense satisfaction to all members of the Royal College of Music."

B305.Howells, H. "Sir Arthur Bliss." <u>Three-Choirs Festival Handbook</u>, Gloucester, 1971, p.8.

A tribute to Bliss in his 80th year, with recollections of earlier festivals, especially 1922.

B306.Howes, F. "Bliss's Music for String Orchestra." <u>The Musical Times</u>, 77 (April 1936), pp.305-8.

A very detailed analysis of <u>Music for Strings</u>, together with copious musical examples. <u>See</u>: W25

B307.Howes, F. "The creative personality of Sir Arthur Bliss." <u>The Times</u> (London), 29 July 1966, p.8.

"...a bird's eye survey (of Bliss's life and music) which makes no attempt to be a critical summary of a lifetime's work, which indeed would be out of place on a birthday greeting card, but it may serve as a fitting retrospect of positive achievement to

be contemplated with pride and pleasure at this
moment ...."

B308.Howes, F. "Sir Arthur Bliss." <u>Music in Britain: A</u>
<u>Quarterly Review</u>, no.48 (Spring 1960), pp.4-6.

A brief synopsis of Arthur Bliss's life, with
mention of the main works. "Sir Arthur Bliss is...
an eminent English composer of distinction, a
cultivated man ... a respected figurehead of the
musical profession ... a worthy ambassador of
English culture ... and a healthy influence in
English music."

B309.Hughes, H. "Music and Musicians." <u>The Saturday Review</u>,
31 December 1932, p.691.

A mention of Arthur Bliss, prompted by the first
performance of the <u>Clarinet Quintet</u>, "...a
masterpiece of rare distinction, so beautifully
made that one is immediately aware that it contains
not a note too little or a note too much." See:
W55a

B310.Hughes, Patrick. "The Younger English Composers: IV -
Arthur Bliss." <u>Monthly Musical Record</u>, LIX (May
1929), pp.129-131.

A general survey of Bliss's life and music,
together with a chronological list of works,
compiled by the composer.

B311.Hull, R.H. "Arthur Bliss : A Revolutionary Finds
Himself." <u>The Musical Mirror</u>, March 1930, p.49.

An account of Bliss's music, prompted by "the
inclusion of ... <u>Introduction and Allegro</u> ... in
the programme of the BBC Symphony Concert at the
Queen's Hall ... which forms one of several
agreeable indications that this composer's just
claims to attention are being accorded increasing
recognition."

B312.Hull, R.H. "Bliss's Colour Symphony re-considered."
<u>Monthly Musical Record</u>, Ll (July 1931), p.200.

A re-examination of the <u>Colour Symphony</u>, in light
of Bliss's revisions to the score. <u>See</u>: W10e

B313.Hull, R.H. "The Colour of Bliss's Symphony." <u>The</u>
<u>Musical Mirror and Fanfare</u>, July-August 1932,
pp.136-7.

The author's objection to a descriptive title for
Bliss's symphony, as proposed by Mr. Percy Scholes.

B314.Hull. R.H. "Morning Heroes." <u>Radio Times</u>, 30 January
1931, p.233.

An introduction to <u>Morning Heroes</u>, for listeners to the radio. <u>See</u>: W84b

B315.Hull, R.H. "The Music fo Arthur Bliss." <u>The Chesterian</u>, no.122 (July/August 1935), pp.153-7.

An article dealing with Bliss's music, up to the <u>Viola Sonata</u> which "... can convince the listener of its striking power and inventive splendour, and emphasise... the exceptional interest to be expected for Bliss's achievements within the next decade."

B316.Huntley. John. "British Film Composers : Arthur Bliss." <u>Music Parade</u>, 1 (1949), pp.9-11 and 16.

An account of Bliss's film music, concentrating on <u>Things to Come</u>, <u>Men of Two Worlds</u> and <u>Christopher Columbus</u>. <u>See</u>: W134, W136, W139

B317.J.,R. "Gunfire music - and a rebuke." <u>Daily Express</u> (London), 17 September 1946, p.3.

A review of the concert suite for <u>Adam Zero</u>, directed by Constant Lambert who "... conducted a warlike performance." <u>See</u>: W46

B318.Jacobs, Arthur. "The Enchantress." <u>The Musical Times</u>, 93 (May 1952), p.224.

A mention of the first public performance of <u>The Enchantress</u>, sung by Katheleen Ferrier in the Royal Festival Hall. <u>See</u>: 78b

B319.Jefferson, Alan. "Arthur Bliss: a souvenir." <u>Le Grand Baton: Journal of the Sir Thomas Beecham Society</u>, 14 (March 1977), pp.10,16-17.

An appreciation of Bliss's life and music.

B320.Jefferson, Alan. "Bliss: composer royal." <u>Music and Musicians</u>, October 1965, pp.26-7,29 and 54.

A detailed article about the composer's music, together with a list of works in chronological order.

B321.Johnston, L. "Sir Arthur Bliss." <u>The New York Times</u>, 11 January 1975, p.19.

A report that "... Sir Arthur Bliss will conduct an orchestra today for the last time before retiring at 83 on physician's orders."

B322.Keller, Hans. "Four aspects of Music." <u>The Composer</u>, no.22 (Winter 1966/7), pp.16-17.

An interview in which Bliss is asked what he wants from music - quality of sound, the question of the logic and flow of the musical thought, the kind of communication and finally the value of the personality in music.

B323.Kennedy, M. "Minor men with major works." The Daily Telegraph (Manchester edition), 3 May 1980, p.15.

A brief article about such English composers as Gerald Finzi, now overlooked and neglected, with a mention of Arthur Bliss who "... is in danger at present of also being overlooked much as Finzi has been."

B324.Kennedy, M. "New Bliss Work at Birmingham." The Musical Times, 97 (February 1956), pp.92-3.

A review of the first performance of Meditations, a work "... which should be welcomed by orchestras. Its meaning is plain, it is written with the characteristic skill and craftsmanship which Bliss's admirers expect ... and its appeal to the public should be strong." See: W22a

B325.Kennedy, M. "Two British Composers." Halle (Manchester), no.91 (December 1956), pp.1-3.

A general article about the lives and music of Arthur Bliss and Edmund Rubbra.

B326.Kenyon, N. "Memory of War." The Listener, 114, 7 November 1985, p.38.

An appreciation of the music of Arthur Bliss, especially Morning Heroes.

B327.Keown, E. "At the Play." Punch, 21 September 1949, p.331.

A review of J.B. Priestley's play Summer Day's Dream, "... an idyll with a moral broadly stated and ... a charming work ...." See: W146b

B328.L.,S. "The Three Choirs Festival." The Manchester Guardian, 8 September 1922, p.9.

A detailed account of the concert in Gloucester Cathedral which included Bliss's Colour Symphony. "... Bliss is a young composer of amazing vitality, and is far and away the cleverest writer among the English composers of our time. His invention is fertile, rapid and sure." See: W10a

B329.Lambert, C. "Checkmate." Radio Times, 8 October 1937, p.17.

An analysis of Checkmate, by the conductor of the first performance. "To me it is the most successful of Bliss's scores because it combines in one work so many elements of his character which have previously been presented to us only separately." See: W5

B330.Lancelot. "Matters musical." The Referee (London), 25
     April 1915, p.5.

          A review of the concert which included Bliss's
          Piano Quintet. "The composer has plenty of
          pleasing ideas which are expressed in tuneful
          manner...." See: W50a

B331.Liveing, Edward, "Sir Arthur Bliss." The Queen, 10
     March 1954, pp.44 and 81.

          A portrait of the office of Master of the Queen's
          Musick, and how Arthur Bliss brings to this office
          "... a remarkable combination of musical
          achievement and social aptitude." A mention is
          also made of Trudy Bliss and her achievements,
          including "... literature and broadcasting." The
          author ends by saying "A young Queen has shown wise
          judgement in the choice of her new Master of
          Musick."

B332.Long, Peter. "Sir Arthur Bliss." One-o-Four, 3
     (November 1956), pp.65-6.

          A brief sketch of the composer, with the main
          events of his musical life chronicled.

B333.Lyle, W. "Arthur Bliss." The Bookman, March 1923,
     pp.295-7.

          An article surveying Bliss's life and music up to
          1923, prior to him sailing to the United States of
          America in April of that year.

B334.Lyle, W. "Arthur Bliss." The Bookman, July 1932, p.199.

          An interview with the composer, and mention of the
          Colour Symphony and its revisions which "... has
          meant more than simply taking out so many bars of
          the music... and substituting others for them."
          See:W10

B335.Lyle, W. "Arthur Bliss: a personal impression." Musical
     News and Herald, 3 March 1923, p.207.

          A brief impression of the composer whose "...
          forceful energy ... impresses one as much as the
          frankness of his greeting, and the kindliness of
          his manner."

B336.Lyne, F.M. "The Pilgrimage of Mr. Bliss." Bristol
     Evening World, 8 October 1935.

          An account of Bliss's visit to Bristol in
          connection with the BBC survey, and a criticism of
          the resulting article about musical life in that
          city.

B337.M.,C. "Musical Notes." The Lady, 14 July 1921, p.29.

A review of the Karsavina season at the London
Coliseum that included Bliss's orchestration of
Sinding's <u>Fire Dance</u>, which is described as "very
effective." <u>See</u>: W18a

B338. MacDonald, M.   "Ballet Scores."   <u>Gramophone</u>, 57 (June
     1979), p.42.

A review of the HMV recording (ASD 3687) of the
<u>Adam Zero</u> and <u>Checkmate</u> ballet suites. <u>See</u>: D1,D11

B339. MacDonald, M.   "Belmont Variations."   <u>Gramophone</u>, 54
     (Septmeber 1976), p.410

A review of the EMI Studio Two (TWOX 1053) record-
ing of <u>Belmont Variations</u> and <u>Kenilworth</u>. <u>See</u>:
D5,D29

B340. MacDonald, M.   "Concerto  for  Cello  and  Orchestra."
     <u>Gramophone</u>, 55 (June 1977), pp.41-2.

A review of the HMV recording (ASD 3342) which
included the <u>Cello Concerto</u> and the suite from
<u>Miracle in the Gorbals</u>. <u>See</u>: D17, D37

B341. MacDonald, M.   "Greetings to a City."   <u>The Gramophone</u>,
     48 (April 1971), pp.1632 and 1637.

A review of the Philip Jones Brass Ensemble
recording (SDD 274) on the Decca label, featuring
<u>Greetings to a City</u> amongst other pieces. <u>See</u>: D26

B342. MacDonald, M. "Madame Noy, etc."  <u>Gramophone</u>, 62 (April
     1985), p.1260.

A review of the Nash Ensemble's recording (Hyperion
A  66137)  of  <u>Madame  Noy</u>,  <u>Rhapsody</u>,  <u>Rout</u>,
<u>Conversations</u>, <u>The Women of Yueh</u> and the <u>Oboe
Quintet</u>. <u>See</u>:  D18,D32,D51,D52,D54,D67

B343. MacDonald, M.   "Pastoral."   <u>Gramophone</u>, 63 (November
     1985), p.664.

A review of the Hyperion (A 66175) recording which
included the <u>Pastoral</u>. <u>See</u>:D44

B344. MacKenzie, C. "Editorial."   <u>The Gramophone</u>, 21 (October
     1943), pp.65-6.

A survey of the recorded works of Bliss with
comments from reviews appearing in <u>The Gramophone</u>.

B345. McNaught, W. "Adam Zero."   <u>The Musical Times</u>, 87 (May
     1946), pp.155-6.

An excellent introduction to the ballet which is
described as "... outstanding and attractive ....
The score of <u>Adam Zero</u> is full of ideas ...

intelligible, vivid ideas, ideas in novel rhythm, even romantic ideas." See: W4

B346.McNaught, W. "Bliss's String Quartet [1941]." The Musical Times, 83 (May 1942), p.142.

An account of the String Quartet, with particular reference to style and harmony. Musical examples are provided. See: W53

B347.McNaught, W. "London Concerts." The Musical Times, 79 (May 1938), p.381.

A review of the first performance of Checkmate as an orchestral suite, with Arthur Bliss conducting. See: W5c

B348.McNaught, W. "The Olympians." The Musical Times, 90 (October 1949), pp. 367-8.

A review of The Olympians' first performance at the Royal Opera House, Covent Garden. See: W2a

B349.McNaught, W. "The Promenade Concerts." The Musical Times, 80 (September 1939), p.680-1.

An account of the Piano Concerto's first English performance at a Promenade Concert. See: W11b

B350.Mahony, P. "Sir Arthur Bliss : the California Interlude." Composer, no.40 (Summer 1971), pp.7-9.

Concerning Bliss's stay in Santa Barbara, California between 1923 and 1925.

B351.Mahony, P. "Sir Arthur Bliss : 75th birthday." Composer, no.20 (Summer 1966), p.11.

An informal account of Bliss in California, written by his step-brother.

B352.Mahony, P. "Sir Arthur Bliss in Santa Barbara." Noticias (Santa Barbara Historical Society), XVII (Spring 1971), pp.3-6.

An account of Bliss's life in Santa Barbara.

B353.Maine, B. "Arthur Bliss." Radio Times, 28 August 1931, p. 432.

An appreciation of Bliss's life and music.

B354.Maine, B. "Arthur Bliss: the man and his work." The Morning Post (London), 18 September 1930, p.6.

An extended article describing Bliss's work and the influences on his music.

B355.Maine, B. "Arthur Bliss on modern music." The Monthly Musical Record, June 1934, pp.106-7.

A very enlightening interview with the composer.

B356.Maine, B. "A Colour Symphony." <u>The Daily Telegraph</u> (London), 12 August 1922, p.5.

An introduction to the <u>Colour Symphony</u>, and an article looking forward to the first performance in Gloucester Cathedral with the composer as conductor. <u>See</u>: W10

B357.Mann,W. "Bliss Birthday Concert." <u>The Times</u> (London), 14 July 1971, p.9.

An account of the concert celebrating the 80th birthday of Sir Arthur Bliss.

B358.Mann, W. "British music tests new hall." <u>The Times</u> (London), 3 March 1967, p.10.

A description of the opening of the Queen Elizabeth Hall on the South Bank of the Thames. "Sir Arthur Bliss conducted one item, his own <u>River Music 1967</u>, a deft a cappella choral piece to a poem by Cecil Day Lewis." <u>See</u>: W94a

B359.Mann, W. "Checkmate." <u>The Gramophone</u>, 38 (August 1960), p.130.

A review of the World Record Club (ST52) recording of Bliss conducting various pieces, including his suite from <u>Checkmate</u> and the <u>Set of Act Tunes and Dances</u>. <u>See</u>: D11, D60

B360.Mann, W. "Gold medallist." <u>The Times</u> (London), 15 October 1970, p.11.

A description of the ceremony when Bliss presented the Royal Philharmonic Society's gold medal to Mstislav Rostropovich.

B361.Marcato. "The Rise of Arthur Bliss." <u>The Weekly Dispatch</u> (London), 10 July 1921, p.6.

An informal description of the composer, and an account of his forthcoming engagements.

B362.March, I. "Christopher Columbus." <u>Gramophone</u>. 57 (December 1979), p.1024.

A review of the HMV recording (ASD 3797) of British music for film and television, including the suite from <u>Christopher Columbus</u>. <u>See</u>: D12

B363.March, I. "Processional." <u>Gramophone</u>, 55 (June 1977), p.106.

A review of the recording (HMV: ASD 3341) of some English music, released during Silver Jubilee Year, including <u>Processional</u>. <u>See</u>: D47

B364.Mason, C. "Aubade." The Musical Times, 94 (July 1953), p.327.

A review of the first performance of A Garland to the Queen. See: W74a

B365.Mayer, D.M. "Arthur Bliss." Crescendo, no.13 (February 1948), p.5-6.

A brief profile of the composer, highlighting his liveliness - "... one of Bliss's chief characteristics ... which runs through his whole personality and his work."

B366.Mitchell, D. "Bliss's new violin concerto." The Musical Times, 96 (June 1955), p.324.

A review of the Violin Concerto's first performance, a concerto which "... proved to be large-hearted music, intent ... on making broad lyrical gestures in the romantic manner; the many echoes of Elgar's masterpiece were significant." See: W13a

B367.Mitchell, D. "Songs." The Musical Times, 96 (March 1955), pp.152-3.

A brief mention of the Elegiac Sonnet which "... impressed by its craftsmanship, its elequence and heartfelt lyricism." See: W38a

B368.Neilson, David. "Belmont Variations." The British Bandsman, 28 September 1963, p.3.

A brief paragraph looking forward to the new test piece for the forthcoming Brass Band Championships. See W149

B369.Newman, E. "The association of colour with music." The Graphic, 16 September 1922, p.424.

A discussion at the question of the association of colour with music, which concludes that speculation as to the union between the two will never come to anything. See: W10

B370.Newman, E. "The Olympians." The Sunday Times (London), 2 October 1949, p.2.

The first of two extended articles about The Olympians and British opera. See: W2a

B371.Newman, E. "The Olympians." The Sunday Times (London), 9 October 1949, p.2.

The concluding article about The Olympians and Newman's views on the state of British opera. See: W2a

B372.Newman, E. "The Tempest." <u>The Manchester Guardian</u>, 10 February 1921, p.4.

> "The only music that matters is that of Mr. Arthur Bliss, who, with a fearsome array of kettledrums, has given us a storm in the opening scene that isn't only terrifying in an ingenious way... but has the additional and great merit of reducing the scenery and the actors to their native insignificance. Mr. Bliss has written some music that I should like to hear again ... Mr. Bliss is a young musician of a curiously lively, questioning mind." <u>See</u>: W147a

B373.Oliver, M. "String Quartets." <u>Gramophone</u>, 63 (November 1985), pp. 642 and 647.

> A review of the Delme String Quartet recording, of the Bliss String Quartets, on the Hyperion label, A66178. <u>See</u>:D48, D49

B374.Palmer, C. "Aspects of Bliss." <u>The Musical Times</u>, 112 (August 1971), pp.743-5.

> An interesting and informative article tracing the several characteristics of Bliss's music, "... taking the <u>Colour Symphony</u> of 1921 as a point de depart."

B375.Palmer, C. "Bliss." Sevenoaks, Novello, 1976, 22 pp.

> A short biography of the composer, with the main compositions listed as an appendix.

B376.Palmer, C. "Bliss on Stage and Screen." <u>Musical Opinion</u>, 94 (August 1971), pp.558-561.

> A general accent of Bliss's music for the stage and the screen, written as a tribute for the composer's 80th birthday.

B377.Palmer, C. "Morning Heroes." <u>Gramophone</u>, 52 (March 1975), pp.1687-8.

> A review of the HMV (SAN 365) recording of <u>Morning Heroes</u> which is "... most vivid and faithful." <u>See</u>:D38

B378.Palmer, C. "Memorial Tribute - Sir Arthur Bliss." <u>Crescendo</u>, May 1975, pp.25-6.

> An obituary describing his music and tracing his rise to prominence.

B379.Parsons, M. "Radio." <u>The Musical Times</u>, 110 (February 1969), p.186.

> A review of the <u>The Lady of Shalott</u> and the broadcast of the music which is described as "... rich and colourful...." <u>See</u>: W7c

B380.Parsons, M. "Sir Arthur Bliss." The Listener, 80, 26 December 1968, p.869.

An account of several works, including a brief introduction to the music of The Lady of Shalott. See:W7c

B381.Playfair, N. The Story of the Lyric Theatre, Hammersmith. London, Chatto & Windsor, 1925, pp.31-2, 43-55, 166-168.

Mention of the productions of La Serva Padrona and As You Like It. See: W1, W142b

B382.Porter, A. "The Beatitudes." The Musical Times, 103 (July 1962), p.459.

A review of the concert when The Beatitudes was first performed in May 1962. See: W75a

B383.Porter, A. "Queen Elizabeth Hall." The Musical Times, 108 (April 1967), p.339.

A description of the opening of the QEH with a performance, amongst other things, of River Music 1967 "... an extended partsong to words by C. Day Lewis, weaving the themes of music and the Thames." See: W94a

B384.Powell, D. "Films of the Week." The Sunday Times (London), 21 July 1946, p.2.

A review of new films, including Men of Two Worlds, directed by Thorold Dickinson. See: W136a

B385.Powers, A. "Harmonious Mansions" Country Life, 29 August 1985, pp.559-563.

A fascinating article, with illustrations, about two houses, built by Peter Harland for two composers in the 1930's, one for Gerald Finzi, the other for Sir Arthur Bliss. The results, however, were strikingly different, reflecting the characters of the two clients as much as the ideas of the architects.

B386.Priestley, J.B. "My Friend Bliss." The Musical Times, 112 (August 1971), pp.740-1.

A personal memoir by J.B. Priestley who wrote the libretto for Bliss's opera The Olympians.

B387.Priestley, J.B. "The Olympians." Composer, no.20, (Summer 1966), pp.12-13.

An account of how the libretto for The Olympians was written, together with Priestley's views on the opera. See: W2

B388.R., H.T. "Hailing Mr. Bliss, Saluting Mr. Hill, Clapping Pianists." <u>Boston Evening Transcript</u>, 20 December 1924, p.13.

A detailed report about the first performance of Bliss's <u>Concerto for Two Pianos and Orchestra</u>, in which it is described as "... exhilarating and exciting..." with "... Mr. Bliss at the top of his form ...." <u>See</u>: W12b

B389.R.,P. "Two Novelties on Symphony Program." <u>The Globe</u>, (Boston), 20 December 1924.

A review of the <u>Concerto for Two Pianos and Orchestra's</u> first performance. "This concerto has the rhythmic nervous stidency of Stravinsky's climaxes. The ideas and the musical idiom are ... fresh and vivid." <u>See</u>: W12b

B390.Raleigh, H.M.  "Mr. Priestley's new play is easy to watch." <u>The Yorkshire Post</u> (Leeds), 9 August 1949, p.3.

A review of <u>Summer Day's Dream</u> in which the acting is described as "excellent." <u>See</u>: W146a

B391.Raynor, H.  "Recollections for a Birthday." <u>Daily Telegraph and Morning Post</u>, 29 July 1961, p.9.

An article based on an interview with Sir Arthur Bliss, with his views on certain subjects including English composers.

B392.Redington, S. "King Solomon." <u>The Santa Barbara Press</u>, 22 March 1924.

A review of <u>King Solomon</u>, with music by Bliss which is described as "... bizarre, weird ... written and directed by Arthur Bliss which was not the least part of the effect ...." <u>See</u>: W143a

B393.Rees, C.B.  "Sir Arthur Bliss." <u>Halle</u>, December 1956, p.6.

A brief sketch about the composer, his life and music.

B394.Rees, C.B.  "Sir Arthur Bliss." <u>Musical Events</u>, May 1971, pp.10-11.

An account of the composer's musical career in celebration of his 80th birthday.

B395.Rees, C.B.  "Sir Arthur Bliss : a concert of his music." <u>Musical Events</u>, January 1955, pp.17 and 19.

An introduction to the music of Arthur Bliss, with a description of him as a conductor.

B396.Rees, L. "Music and Musicians." <u>The Sunday Times</u> (London), 25 April 1915, p.4.

A review of the concert which included Bliss's <u>Piano Quartet</u> "... which won warm favour by its wealth of melodic invention and its varied and attractive colouring, despite some weakness and diffuseness of treatment." <u>See</u>: W50a

B397.Reynolds, G. "Organ Music." <u>Gramophone</u> 59 (October 1981), p.584.

A review of the Wealden recording (WS 206) which included Bliss's <u>Praeludium</u>. It is described as "... making effective and restrained use of percussion ... producing a wide range of expression within its roaming framework, from soft and appealing to menacing." <u>See</u>: D45

B398.Richards, D. "Bliss." <u>Music and Musicians</u>, 20 (September 1971) pp.40-3, 46-7.

A detailed synposis of Bliss's life and music, with illustrations and the publication of <u>Sea Love</u> (W112) as an appendix.

B399.Richards, Jeffrey. "Thorold Dickinson - the man and his films." London, Croom Helm, 1986.

Chapter 6, subtitled <u>Emergent Africa : Men of Two Worlds</u>, provides an extremely detailed and fascinating account of the film, its creation and the music. <u>See</u>: W136

B400.Roberts, M. "Arthur Bliss's ballet Miracle in the Gorbals: a study." <u>Music in Education</u>, March-April 1946, pp.8-11.

A detailed study of <u>Miracle in the Gorbals</u>, with copious musical examples. <u>See</u>: W8

B401.Robertson, A. "Arthur Bliss." in Bacharach, A.L. <u>British Music of Our Time</u>, Harmondsworth, Penguin Books, 1951, pp.147-56.

A survey of Bliss's music, with a useful introduction to the songs and choral works.

B402.Robertson, A. "Arthur Bliss - a Composer with a Zest for Life." <u>Radio Times</u>, 10 July 1953, p.29.

A brief article on Bliss "who has enriched the nation's heritage of music."

B403.Robertson,A. "Aubade." <u>The Gramophone</u>, 31 (November 1953), p.203.

A review of the Columbus recording (33CX 1063) of <u>A Garland for the Queen</u>. <u>See</u>: D3.

B404.Robertson, A. "Concerto for Piano and Orchestra." The Gramophone, 31 (November 1953), p.183.

A review of the Nixa (CLP 1167) recording of the Piano Concerto, performed by Noel Mewton-Wood. See:D14

B405.Robertson, Alec. "Hymn to Apollo, etc." The Gramophone 49 (August 1971), p.332.

A review of the Lyrita recording (SRCS 55) which included Hymn to Apollo, A Prayer to the Infant Jesus, Rout, Serenade and The World is Charged. This was the disc, sponsored by the Performing Right Society, presented to the composer on 2 August 1971, his eightieth birthday. See: D27, D46, D54, D59, D68

B406.Robertson, Alec. "A Knot of Riddles." The Gramophone, 48 (November 1970), pp.824 and 829.

A review of the Pye Virtuoso disc TPLS 13036 of A Knot of Riddles and the Pastoral. See: D30,D44

B407.Robertson, Alec. "The music of Arthur Bliss." Philharmonic Post, January/February 1949, p.7.

A brief account of Bliss's music, with the emphasis on his ballet music.

B408.Robertson, Alec. "Quartet for Strings." The Gramophone 29(June 1951), p.8.

A review of the Decca 10" recording (LX 3038) featuring the Griller String Quartet playing Bliss's String Quartet in F minor. See: D49

B409.Robertson, Alec. "Quintet for clarinet, etc." The Gramophone, 41 (October 1963), pp.195-6.

A review of the World Record Club disc of Bliss's clarinet and oboe quintets, played by the Melos Ensemble. See: D50, D51

B410.Rosenthal, H. "The Olympians." Opera, April 1972, pp.379-80.

An account of the revival of The Olympians at the Royal Festival Hall in February 1972. See: W2b

B411.Ross, J. "Special Games Fanfare." The West Australian (Melbourne), 1 August 1962, p.25.

An announcement that Sir Arthur Bliss has written a fanfare to accompany the opening of the Commonwealth Games. It is noted that "Sir Arthur Bliss is the first holder of his office to write special music for an important Commonwealth occasion outside Britain." See: W162

B412. S.,A. "A Symphony by Mr. Arthur Bliss."  The Birmingham
Post, 8 September 1922, p.6.

> A review of the Colour Symphony's first performance
> at    Gloucester.    "Certainly    it    is    the    most
> remarkable work of symphonic proportions produced
> in recent years.  It is a work of a live force, a
> composer to be reckoned with...."  See:W10a

B413. S., H.A. "A Curious Concerto."  The Westminster Gazette,
13 June 1921, p.5.

> An account of the concert when Bliss's Concerto for
> Piano, Tenor voice, Percussion and Strings was
> given its first performance.  "... the pianoforte
> part ...  proved interesting enough... though he
> overdid his xylophone effects badly."  See: W12a

B414. S.,H.A.    "Philharmonic    Quartet."    The    Westminster
Gazette, 26 June 1915.

> A review of the first performance of the String
> Quartet in A which "... proved quite a interesting
> composition.  Mr. Bliss writes easily and effect-
> ively for his instruments, and also has ideas...."
> See: W51d

B415. S.,R.  "Bliss conducting his own music."  The Evening
Mail (Leicester), 13 October 1958.

> A report about the concert version of The Beggar's
> Opera and a performance conducted by Bliss.  "The
> film never had the public recognition it deserved
> and the chance of hearing the musical arrangements
> ... was indeed welcome."  See: W132b

B416. Sadie, S. "The Golden Cantata."  The Musical Times, 105
(April 1964), p.283.

> A review of The Golden Cantata's first performance
> in Cambridge in February 1964.  See: W80a

B417. Sadie, S. "A substantial piece."  The Times (London), 25
June 1970, p.7.

> A description of the Cello Concerto at its first
> performance where it is described as "... a pretty
> substantial piece.  The piece is artfully scored;
> the orchestra is small and textures are kept lucid
> and transparent...."  See: W14a

B418. St. John, C.  "Music: a fruitful week."  Time and Tide
(London), 24 December 1920, p.689.

> An account of Grace Crawford singing Rout "... an
> amazing piece of orchestral writing in miniature.
> Rout was received with such enthusiam that it had
> to be repeated and, "by request" was given a third
> time at the end of the concert."  See:W118a

B419.St. John,C. "Music: Public Taste." <u>Time and Tide</u> (London), 22 July 1921, p.701.

> A review of London concerts including the Karsavina season at the Coliseum." ... Bliss's orchestration of the Sinding <u>Fire Dance</u> is excellent and Karsavina's dancing admirable ...." <u>See</u>:W18a

B420.St. John,C. "Music: Singers with Ideas." <u>Time and Tide</u>, 15 October 1920, p.471.

> Bliss's <u>Rhapsody</u> is described as "...very entertaining...," and the instrumental colour "...gives his music a much more weird effect." <u>See</u>: W116a

B421.Salter, L. "Colour Symphony." <u>The Gramophone</u>, 34 (August 1956), p.81.

> A review of the Decca recording (LXT 5170) of the <u>Colour Symphony</u> and <u>Introduction and Allegro</u>. <u>See</u>: D13,D28

B422.Salter, L. "Colour Symphony." <u>Gramophone</u>, 55 (November 1977), pp.829-830.

> A review of the EMI disc (ASD 3416) of the <u>Colour Symphony</u> and the suite of <u>Things to Come</u>, arranged by Christopher Palmer. <u>See</u>: D13,D63

B423.Salter, L. "Concerto for Violin and Orchestra." <u>The Gramophone</u>, 34 (June 1956), p.7.

> A review of the Decca disc (LXT 5166) featuring the <u>Violin Concerto</u> and <u>Theme and Cadenza</u> (Memorial Concert). <u>See</u>: D16, D36

B424.Salter, L. "Things to Come." <u>Gramophone</u>, 54 (June 1976), pp.95-6.

> A review of a disc (Decca PFS 4363) devoted to British film music and including the Suite from <u>Things to Come</u>. <u>See</u>: D63

B425.Scholes, P.A. "The Bliss Colour Symphony." <u>The Observer</u> (London), 11 March 1923, p.6.

> A reaction to the first London performance of the <u>Colour Symphony</u> which is described as "...rhythmically vital, melodically interesting and masterly in orchestration...." <u>See</u>: W10b

B426.Scholes, P.A. "Bliss and Stravinsky." <u>The Observer</u> (London), 10 July 1921, p.10.

> A report of Bliss's lecture to the Society of Women Musicians.

B427.Scholes, P.A. "A Colour Symphony." <u>The Observer</u> (London), 30 July 1922, p.9.

An analytical introduction to Bliss's <u>Colour Symphony</u>, with musical examples. "The orchestration looks interesting... my general impression is that the work has a greal deal of vitality about it." <u>See</u>: W10

B428. Scholes, P.A. "A few notes upon the work of Arthur Bliss and espcially upon this Colour Symphony." London, Goodwin and Tabb, 1922.

An essay on Bliss's music and an introduction to the <u>Colour Symphony</u>. <u>See</u>: W10

B429. Scholes, P.A. "Music of the Week". <u>The Observer</u> (London), 16 October 1921, p.10.

A criticism of <u>Melee Fantasque</u> after its first performance. "... my present criticism of the piece is that it is too broken, and contains passages which appear to be more interpolations included to show us some orchestral possibility." <u>See</u>: W23a

B430. Scholes, P.A. "Music of the Week." <u>The Observer</u> (London), 20 February 1921, p.8.

A review of the first performance of <u>Two Studies</u>, one of which "...was... striking." <u>See</u>: W30a

B431. Scholes, P.A. "The Title of Bliss's Colour Symphony." <u>The Musical Times</u>, 73 (May 1932), pp.416-7.

A reply to an article and discussion about the association of colour and music. <u>See</u>: W10c

B432. Scholes, P.A. "Yesterday's Music." <u>The Observer</u> (London), 12 June 1921, p.16.

An article about Bliss's <u>Concerto for Piano and Tenor Voice</u>. "What is strong about this new piece is its vigour... the whole thing has force and character." <u>See</u>: W12a

B433. Shawe-Taylor, D. "Festival of Bliss." <u>The Sunday Times</u> (London), 11 July 1976, p.32.

An account of the 1976 Cheltenham Festival which featured Bliss's music.

B434. Shawe-Taylor, D. "Death of a Poet." <u>The Sunday Times</u> (London), 30 March 1975, p.35.

A tribute to Bliss "... in whose death ... English music has sustained a whole chapter of losses. No better Master of the Queen's Music could gave been found. If his appearance and manner were those of a cheerful and capable retired colonel, his soul was that of an English poet."

B435. Storey Smith, W. "Pianists Jazz with Symphony." <u>The Post</u> (Boston). 20 December 1924.

The <u>Concerto for Two Pianos and Orchestra</u> is described as "... disdaining accepted canons of beauty. It is empty and dull." <u>See</u>: W12b

B436.Tertis, Lionel. "My Viola and I." London, Paul Elek, 1974, p.74.

A description of the first-ever performance of the <u>Viola Sonata</u> by Tertis and Solomon with William Walton turning the pages. <u>See</u>: W60a

B437.Thompson, K.L. "Arthur Bliss: catalogue of works." <u>The Musical Times</u>, 107 (August 1966), pp.666-673.

A lot of Bliss's works, together with a bibliography and discography.

B438.Thompson, K.L. "Bliss: Supplement to the Catalogue of Works." <u>The Musical Times</u>, 112 (August 1971), pp.745-6.

A list of additional facts to the original list, together with a section on more recent works.

B439.Toye, F. "Music and Musicians." <u>The Morning Post</u> (London), 21 January 1936, p.16.

A review of Bliss's articles on his BBC tour, with mention of the impression made on him by choral societies and brass bands.

B440.Turbet, R. and Mooney, B. "A True Artist Who is kindly, elegant and witty." <u>Pi</u>, 2 November 1976, p.8.

The results of a brief interview with Bliss, with his views on other composers. "He is a fascinating man, a man of vision ... with Edward Elgar, Sir Arthur Bliss is undoubtedly the most significant composer to hold the post of Master of the Queen's Musick."

B441.Vogel, A. "Bliss's Meditations." <u>The Chesterian</u>, XXXII (Autumn 1957), pp.55-6.

An analysis of <u>Meditations on a Theme by John Blow</u>, movement by movement. <u>See</u>:W22

B442.Wallis, G. "Tobias and the Angel." <u>The Musical Times</u>, 101 (July 1960), p.432.

A brief review of Bliss's television opera <u>Tobias and the Angel</u>, tramsitted in May 1960. <u>See</u>: W3a

B443.Walsh, S. "Master of Musick." <u>The Observer</u> (London), 30 March 1975, p.4.

An obituary in which Bliss is described as "... one of the most vigorous and independent-minded British composers of his generation - very far removed from

the stuffy image many people have of the appointment he held for the last 22 years."

B444.Walsh, S. "Processional." Gramophone, 55 (October
1977), p.712.

A review of the recording (VPS 1055) of
Processional, arranged for organ by Garrett
O'Brien. See D47

B445.Warrack, J. "Mastering the Queen's Musick." The Sunday
Telegraph (London), 30 July 1961, p.9.

An appreciation of Bliss and his music, with
mention of the duties of Master of the Queen's
Musick.

B446.Warrack, J. "Sonata for Piano." Gramophone, 52 (February
1975), p.1516.

A review of the Argo disc (ZRG 786) featuring the
Piano Sonata. See: D61

B447.Webber, J.L. "Performers' Platform." Composer, no.55
(Summer 1975), pp.11-13.

A commentary on developments in 'cello technique
and repertoire from Prokofiev to the present day,
including the Bliss Cello Concerto.

B448.Webster, E.M.  "The Olympians." Musical Opinion, 95
(April 1972), pp.347-8.

An account of the concert at the Royal Festival
Hall which including a revival of The Olympians.
See: W2b

B449.Willcocks, D. "Obituary : Arthur Bliss." Royal College
of Music Magazine, LXXI (Summer Term, 1975),
pp.39-41.

A transcript of the address, delivered by David
Willcocks at the Memorial Service on 20 May 1975.

B450.Wimbush, R. "Investiture." The Gramophone, 47 (September
1969), pp. 445-6.

A review of the official recording (Delyse SROY1)
of the Investiture of Prince Charles as Prince of
Wales at Caernafon Castle. See: D39

B451.Winnington, Richard. "In Darkest Denham." News
Chronicle (London), 20 July 1946, p.2.

A review of Men of Two Worlds with particular
mention of the music. "... to be praised without
qualification is the musical score of Arthur Bliss
...." See: W136a

B452.Woodward, J. "Bliss: the human element."  Christian
     Science Monitor, 13 August 1969, p.6.

          A brief chronicle of Bliss's career, ranging over
          50 years of music.

B453.Woodward, I. "The sound of musick."  The Guardian
     (Manchester), 26 July 1969, p.7.

          An appreciation on Bliss's 78th birthday, with
          mention of his career and his views on electronic
          music which "... has a great future ahead of it
          ...."

B454.Wortham, H.E. "Arthur Bliss."  The Sackbut, April 1927,
     pp.251-5.

          A detailed commentary on Bliss's life and early
          music, up to the Colour Symphony.

B455.Wortham, H.E. "Music and Colour."  The Morning Post
     (London), 6 September 1922, p.5.

          A discussion as to whether music and colour are
          related, prompted by the appearance of Bliss's
          Colour Symphony.

B456.XXX. "London Concerts."  The Musical Times, 69 (November
     1928), p.1034.

          A review of some Promenade "novelties" including
          "Mr. Bliss's ... Double Fugue from his Colour
          Symphony ... which the audience acclaimed with
          joy." See: W10d

# Appendix I:
# Alphabetical List
# of Main Compositions

Numbers following each title, e.g. W152, refer to the "Works
and Performances" section of this volume.

Adam Zero, W4
An Age of Kings, W141
Allegro [for strings], W33
Andante Tranquillo e Legato, W34
Angels of the Mind, W106
As you like it, W142
At the Window, W107
Aubade for Coronation Morning, W74
Auvergnat, W108

The Ballads of the Four Seasons, W109
The Beatitudes, W75
The Beggar's Opera, W132
The Belmont Variations, W149
A Birthday Greeting, W9
Birthday Greetings to the Croydon Symphony Orchestra, W150
Birthday Song for a Royal Child, W76
Bliss: One Step, W35

Caesar and Cleopatra, W133
Call to Adventure, W151
Ceremonial Prelude, W152
Checkmate, W5
A Child's Prayer, W110
Choral Prelude: Das Alte Jahre, W36
Christopher Columbus, W134
A Colour Symphony, W10
Concerto for Piano and Orchestra, W11
Concerto for Piano, Tenor Voice, Strings and Percussion, W12
Concerto for Violin and Orchestra, W13
Concerto for Violoncello and Orchestra, W14
Conquest of the Air, W135
Conversations, W37
Cradle Song for Newborn Child, W77

Mortlake, W85
Music for the Investiture of the Prince of Wales, W167
Music for A Prince, W46
Music for a Service of the Order of the Bath, W168
Music for Strings, W25
Music for the Wedding of HRH Princess Alexandra, W169
Music for the Wedding of HRH Princess Anne, W170
Music for the Wedding of HRH Princess Margaret, W171

O Give Thanks, W86
Ode for Sir William Walton, W87
The Olympians, W2
One, two, buckle my shoe, W88


Pastoral, W89
Peace Fanfare, W172
Pen Selwood, W90
The Phoenix, W26
Play a Penta, W47
Praeludium, W48
Prayer to St. Francis of Assisi, W91
A Prayer to the Infant Jesus, W92
Prelude for Brass, W173
Presence au Combat, W137
Processional, W27
Put thy trust in the Lord, W93

Quartet for piano, clarinet, cello and timpani, W49
Quartet for piano and strings, W50
Quartet No 1 for strings, W51
Quartet No 2 for strings, W52
Quartet No 3 for strings, W53
Quartet No 4 for strings, W54
Quintet for clarinet and strings, W55
Quintet for oboe and strings, W56
Quintet for piano and strings, W57

Rhapsody, W116
Rich or Poor, W114
River Music, W94
Rout, W118
The Rout Trot, W58
The Royal Palaces of Great Britain, W145

Sailing or Flying?, W119
Salute to Lehigh University, W174
Salute to Painting, W175
Salute to the Royal Society, W176
Salute to Shakespeare, W177
Santa Barbara, W95
Seek the Lord, W96
Serenade, W97
La Serva Padrona, W1
Set of Act Tunes and Dances, W28
Seven American Poems, W120
Seven Waves Away, W138
Shield of Faith, W98
Signature and Interlude Tune for ABC TV, W29
Simples, W121

Sing Mortals, W99
Sonata for piano, W59
Sonata for viola and piano, W60
Sonata for violin and piano, W61
Song of Welcome, W100
Spirit of the Age, W178
Stand Up and Bless the Lord, W101
Study for solo piano, W62
Suite for piano (c.1912), W63
Suite for piano (1925), W64
Summer Day's Dream, W146

The Tempest, W147
Things to Come, W139
Three Bach Chorales, W179
Three Jolly Gentlemen, W122
Three Jubilant and Three Solemn Fanfares, W180
Three Romantic Songs, W123
Three Songs, W124
Three Songs for girls' or boys' voices, W102
'Tis time I think, W125
Toast to the Royal Household, W65
Tobias and the Angel, W3
Toccata for piano, W66
The Tramps, W126
Trio for piano, clarinet and cello, W67
Triptych W68
Tulips, W127
Two American Poems, W128
Two Ballads, W103
Two Fanfares for Let the People Sing, W181
Two Interludes for piano, W69
Two Nursery Rhymes, W129
Two Pieces for clarinet and piano, W70
Two Studies for Orchestra, W30
Twone the House of Felicity, W31

Valse Fantastiques, W71
Valse Melancolique ..., W72

War in the Air, W148
A Wedding Suite, W73
Welcome the Queen, W140
When I was one and twenty, W130
When wilt thou save, W104
The Women of Yueh, W131
The World is Charged, W105

Your questions answered, W32

# Appendix II:
# Chronological List
# of Main Compositions

Numbers following each title, eg. W152, refer to the "Works
and Performances" section of this volume.

1904        Quartet for Piano, Clarinet, Cello and Timpani, W49

1907        March and Valse des Fleurs, W42
              Trio for Piano, Clarinet and Cello, W67

1910        May-Zeeh, W44
              Valse Melancolique ..., W72

1912        Intermezzo, W40
              Suite for Piano, W63

1913        Valse Fantastiques, W71

1914        Quartet No 1 for Strings, W51
              Sonata for Violin and Piano, W61
              'Tis Time I Think, W125

1915        The Hammers, W113
              Quartet for Piano and Strings, W50

1916        Fugue for String Quartet, W39
              The Tramps, W16
              Two Pieces for Clarinet and Piano, W70

1918        Madam Noy, W115
              La Serva Padrona, W1

1919        As You Like It, W142
              Quintet for Piano and Strings, W57
              Rhapsody, W116
              Set of Act Tunes and Dances, W28

1920        Conversations, W37
              Rout, W118
              Two Nursery Rhymes, W129

Two Studies for Orchestra, W30

1921    Concerto for piano, tenor voice, strings and percussion, W12
Fanfare for a Political Address, W158
Fire Dance, W18
Mêlee Fantasque, W23
The Tempest, W147
Three Romantic Songs, W123

1922    A Colour Symphony, W10
Three Songs, W124

1923    The Ballads of the Four Seasons, W109
Bliss, One Step, W35
Elizabethan Suite, W17
Three Jolly Gentlemen, W122
Twone, the House of Felicity, W31
The Women of Yueh, W131

1924    Allegro for Strings, W33
The Fallow Deer at the Lonely House, W111
King Solomon, W143
Masks, W43
Quartet No 2 for Strings, W52
When I was One and Twenty, W130

1925    At the Window, W107
Suite for Piano, W64
Toccata for Piano, W66
Two Interludes for Piano, W69

1926    A Child's Prayer, W110
Hymn to Apollo, W19
Introduction and Allegro, W20
Rich or Poor, W117

1927    Andante Tranquillo e Legato, W34
Thê Festival of Flora, W6
Four Songs, W112
Quintet for oboe and strings, W56
The Rout Trot, W58
Study for solo piano, W62

1928    Pastoral, W89

1929    Serenade, W97

1930    Fanfare for Heroes, W156
Morning Heroes, W84

1932    Choral Prelude: Das Alte Jahr, W36
Quintet for clarinet and strings, W55
Simples, W121

1933    Sonata for viola and piano, W60

1935    Music for Strings, W25
Things to Come, W139
Three Jubilant and Three Solemn Fanfares, W180

1957    Discourse for Orchestra, W15

1958    The Lady of Shalott, W7

1959    Birthday Song for a Royal Child, W76
        Tobias and the Angel, W3

1960    An Age of Kings, W141
        Music for the Wedding of HRH Princess Margaret,
        W171
        Salute to the Royal Society, W176
        Stand up and Bless the Lord, W101
        Three Bach Chorales, W179
        Two Fanfares for Let the People Sing, W181

1961    The Beatitudes, W75
        Call to Adventure, W151
        Greetings to a City, W163
        Toast to the Royal Household, W65

1962    The Belmont Variations, W149
        Gala Fanfare, W162
        March of Homage, W21
        Mary of Magdala, W83

1963    Cradle Song for a Newborn Child, W77
        Golden Cantata, W80
        High Sheriff's Fanfare, W164
        A Knot of Riddles, W114
        Music for the Wedding of HRH Princess Alexandra,
        W169

1964    The Linburn Air, W166
        Salute to Shakespeare, W177

1965    Ceremonial Prelude, W152
        Fanfare for the Commonwealth Arts Festival, W154
        Fanfare:  The Right of the Line, W159
        O Give Thanks Unto the Lord, W86

1966    River Music, W94
        The Royal Palaces of Great Britain, W145

1967    Pen Selwood, W90
        Santa Barbara, W95
        Three Songs for Girls' and Boys' Voices, W102

1968    Angels of the Mind, W106
        Enid's Blast, W153
        Lord, Who shall Abide, W81
        One, Two, Buckle My Shoe, W88
        A Prayer to the Infant Jesus, W92
        Salute to Lehigh University, W174

1969    God Save the Queen, W79
        Miniature Scherzo, W45
        Mortlake, W85
        Music for the Investiture of the Prince of Wales,
        W167
        The World is Charged, W105

1970    Concerto for violoncello and orchestra, W14
        Music for a Prince, W46
        Sailing or Flying, W119
        Triptych, W68
        Tulips, W127
        Two Ballads, W103

1971    Birthday Greetings to the Croydon Symphony
        Orchestra, W150
        Play a Penta, W47
        Praeludium, W48
        Prayer of St. Francis of Assisi, W91

1972    Metamorphic Variations, W24
        Ode to Sir William Walton, W87
        Put Thou Thy Trust in the Lord, W93

1973    Fanfare for the National Fund for Research into
        Crippling Diseases, W157
        Mar Portuguese, W82
        Music for the Wedding of HRH Princess Anne, W170
        A Wedding Suite, W73

1974    Prelude for Brass, W173
        Shield of Faith, W98
        Sing Mortals!, W99
        Spirit of the Age, W178

# Index

Numbers, e.g. p.3, refer to pages in the "Biography";
numbers preceded by a "W" refer to the "Works and
Performances" section; numbers preceded by a "D" to the
"Discography" and numbers preceded by a "B" to the
"Bibliography".

**About the Author**

STEWART R. CRAGGS is the Readers Services Librarian at Sunderland Polytechnic Library in Sunderland, U.K. He is the author of *William Alwyn: A Catalogue of His Music* and *Sir William Walton: A Thematic Catalogue.* He has also published articles in *Perspectives in Music* and *Musical Times.*